STEWARDSHIP
MOTIVES OF THE HEART

STEWARDSHIP
MOTIVES OF THE HEART

JOHN MATHEWS

Pacific Press®
Publishing Association

Nampa, Idaho | Oshawa, Ontario, Canada
www.pacificpress.com

Cover design resources from Lars Justinen

The author assumes full responsibility for the accuracy of all facts and quotations as cited in this book.

Additional copies of this book can be obtained by calling toll-free 1-800-765-6955 or by visiting http://www.adventistbookcenter.com.

ISBN 978-0-8163-6281-3

November 2017

Contents

Introduction

Clayton M. Christensen, a business author, observed that many of his classmates had failed at life management over the years. He concluded, "They didn't keep the purpose of their lives front and center as they decided how to spend their time, talents, and energy."[1]

Do we keep the purpose of our lives front and center? Do we know what it is? I believe the answer is found in a topic that some call boring or irrelevant but is actually very important to our spiritual lives.

We live in a world filled with chaos and selfishness. Even some who go to church think, unconsciously, *What's in it for me?* Some people search for inner peace while refusing to be accountable and believing that spirituality without obligation is the way to go, while others are willing to take a second look at the principles the Bible sets forth regarding the identity of a steward and what *stewardship* might mean for them. We want to be stewards who know how to live, behave, and give in a world of chaos, so that ultimately our life is lived with freedom.

The outcome of good stewardship is a life of "godliness with contentment . . . the true secret of happiness."[2] But this takes spiritual discipline, effort, work, commitment, and accountability—precisely what the culture around us and most of the world are against. These responsible actions and decisions are made to look foolish and irrelevant, arising from principles written by fabulists, for people to use as crutches, for the ones who are not intelligent enough to recognize there is no God. However, for us as believers, reaching our destiny of heaven depends on a correct understanding of stewardship.

As all-encompassing as the topic of stewardship is, there is one common denominator in all its subtopics: stewardship touches everything we do, everything we are, and everything we have.

Someone once said that material things are God's only competitor. Jesus described it this way, "No one can serve two masters. Either you will hate the one and love the other, or you will be devoted to the one and despise the other. You cannot serve both God and money" (Matthew 6:24).

Money has always been a problem for God's people, and modern consumerism isn't helping. This book is about the management of our possessions, about our relationship with money, and about the ways we relate to God as the Owner of all we have.

Of all the varied topics that stewardship includes, why should we focus on money, possessions, wealth, and giving? Two reasons will get us started.

First, at this time in history, people's wealth and their love of money are the greatest threats to God's church fulfilling its mission. Money *is* God's competitor. A number of studies show that people who claim to be Christians continue to give less and less while other priorities take more of their financial resources. What will it take to reverse the trend?

Second, how do we relate, rich or poor, to all the possessions money can buy? Do they reveal anything about our salvation? Gene A. Getz gives us a supracultural principle. A supracultural principle from the Bible can apply at any time in history, anywhere in the world, and within any cultural context. Regarding possessions, he writes, "One of the most significant ways saving faith is tested as to its validity and reality is the way in which professing Christians view and use their material possessions."[3] Then he refers to James 2:17, which says, "Faith by itself, if it is not accompanied by action, is dead." Finally, Getz comments,

Introduction

"This is significant since the way we use our material possessions is the very illustration James used to test whether or not a professing Christian is truly saved."[4]

Let's start the journey to see how we can be successful, relevant, and happy in managing our tangible and intangible possessions for God's glory. We wish to hear one day, "Well done, good and faithful servant! You have been faithful with a few things; I will put you in charge of many things. Come and share your master's happiness!" (Matthew 25:23).

---

1. Clayton M. Christensen, "How Will You Measure Your Life?" in *On Managing Yourself* (Boston: Harvard Business School, 2010), 5.

2. Ellen G. White, *Testimonies for the Church* (Mountain View, CA: Pacific Press®, 1948), 1:542.

3. Gene A. Getz, *A Biblical Theology of Material Possessions* (Eugene, OR: Wipf and Stock,1990), 174.

4. Ibid.

CHAPTER 1

The Influence of Materialism

Max Martin[1] leaned back in his plush office chair, savoring the moment. The computer printout in his hand told the story—a very good story. His construction business had been doing well, and his financial investments were paying off handsomely. He had worked hard—very hard—to put himself and his business on the map. He took advantage of financial situations to improve his position. He wanted it all regardless of who he stepped on to get it. And now it was time to enjoy the fruits of his labors.

Of course, he'd need to reinvest much of his earnings to avoid higher taxes, he reminded himself. But this would be a good time to move his business headquarters from the small second-floor office to a larger, more central location—a suite that would let the world know that he had arrived.

A smile crept across his face as he thought about his new Corvette and the condo on the beach. All the things he had accumulated needed a better place, so now his family could start looking for that bigger home they clamored for—one that would include a pool and tennis court. If only the church would stop nagging him for money, reminding him that God wanted 10 percent plus freewill offerings. He would not mind giving if they would manage the money better.

He reached for his phone and called his investment advisor.

This would be a good year, a very good year. He had worked so hard for so long. He had sacrificed time with his family, grabbing meals on the run, often meeting clients well into the night. Now he could let others do the hard work while he reaped the rewards.

Two days later, the newspaper carried the story. Max Martin had died of a heart attack. The story recounted how he had enjoyed the good things of life. His estate consisted of seven properties, a vintage car collection, and his prize racehorse named Generosity. But now he was gone; his dreams had turned to ashes.

Materialism

Thanks to modern technology, materialism has brought the wonder of "getting stuff" to the most remote parts of the world. However, psychological studies of financial status in different cultures have shown in every case that "materialists were less satisfied with their family, their friends, their self-perception, where they lived, their health, the amount of fun and enjoyment they experienced, the money they made, and their jobs."[2]

While possessions can affect us negatively, living a simple life offers at least two major benefits: freedom and the opportunity to give. These benefits strengthen our relationships and turn our attention from ourselves to others.

One of Merriam-Webster's definitions for materialism is "a way of thinking that gives too much importance to material possessions rather than to spiritual or intellectual things." The possessions that we have acquired often determine our sense of status and the actual value system we live by. So that you understand better what we are grappling with, here are seven essential features of materialism defined.

1. Money. Materialism is the result of our love affair with money. There is no limit to greed and covetousness, and it can have a numbing influence on a Christian. Money is the façade that hides Satan's true identity. He has elevated it so that people make it the god of this world; but it is only a demigod. It has power but not ultimate power.

When a person handles money, their brain produces the same

chemical that is produced when a person takes drugs. People fight for money, gamble to get it, and lie, cheat, and steal to hold on to it. Some call it "brain candy," and they just can't get enough of this artificial sweet, because with it they can buy stuff. They imagine it will make them secure. People, rich and poor alike, spend their lives chasing the dream of prosperity. Some attain it, but many spend their lives wishing for it.

2. Consumerism. If materialism is the religion, then consumerism is the sanctuary in which we meet to worship. Consumerism is the never-ending cycle of acquiring more stuff. We never get enough, no matter how much we have. Just observe houses in different neighborhoods. Some have no garage, while others have a one-car, two-car, or three-car garage—all full of stuff. Storage units are packed with possessions, much of it simply junk. Homes are full to capacity. Yet retailers want us to buy more.

Retailers are very good at separating us from our money. They want each of us to become a consumer from the cradle to the grave. They use every method known to understand our purchasing whims and work nonstop to make us want more—now. They know that if we don't buy right now, we might not buy. Giving customers what they want is achieved by mass-producing products with the ability of individual customization. One example is the smartphone, which is almost endlessly customizable.

Consumerism is often moralized and spiritualized as a positive idea, but it is the mechanism that keeps a dangerous materialism alive. Consumerism promises (falsely) that possessions will bring us happiness, success, social status, and an affluence-enhanced individuality.

Accumulating possessions is not new. The rich young ruler could not bear to part with his possessions (Matthew 19:16–22). Lot's wife left her possessions, the accumulated wealth of many years, in Sodom, along with her heart (Genesis 19:26). "She rebelled against God because His judgments involved her possessions and her children in the ruin. . . . She presumptuously looked back [to Sodom] to desire the life of those who had rejected the divine warning."[3]

The New English Translation draws attention to the power of

possessions. "Because all that is in the world (the desire of the flesh and the desire of the eyes and the arrogance produced by material possessions) is not from the Father, but is from the world" (1 John 2:16, NET). In comparison, think of Job. He was wealthy, but he never allowed possessions, or a lack thereof, to destroy his relationship with God.

3. Television. People watch a lot of television. Some research indicates that it cuts the average life span for women by 1.5 years and for men by 1.8 years.[4] While television can be a wonderful tool in the work of the Lord, it also can be the evangelistic arm of materialism.

In the 1950s, the components of consumerism were set: a home, vehicles, retailers, and television. The home needed possessions, the retailers had the products, television advertised the products, and the vehicle provided the means to get the products to the house. Now there are hundreds of channels on which retailers are able to market products. Perhaps someday, drones will deliver them to your house.

Advertising reaches us through our senses—our eyes and ears. The images are attractive, the words are chosen carefully, and the music is specifically chosen to make a product enticing. Advertisers use jingles with humor and surprise and other ways to attract and hold our attention for a brief period of time. Products are branded by playing the commercial over and over. Retailers consider their brand successful when all they have to do is show a logo, as in Starbucks or Coca Cola, and people recognize the product.

Advertising affects the amount of junk food eaten, alcohol consumed, and many other aspects of how we live. Especially harmful is the influence on the young, who see about 40,000 commercials per year, according to the journal *Pediatrics*.[5] The danger is that children can't always discern between reality and fantasy because their cognitive powers are not fully developed. Commercials are a small but influential part of viewing habits. It is important that we follow David's counsel, "I will not look with approval on anything that is vile. I hate what faithless people do; I will have no part in it" (Psalm 101:3).

14

4. Sensuality. Satan adds glamour to lure people down an attractive road that numbs them to eternal realities. No other story in the Bible demonstrates the sensual side of materialism better than that of Sodom and Gomorrah. Ellen White explains the link. "There is nothing more desired among men than riches and leisure, and yet these gave birth to the sins that brought destruction upon the cities of the plain."[6]

Looking at sensual things influences our thoughts and actions. However, "one of the main reasons individuals have unrealistic ideals about wealth and possessions is that they frequently view such images in the media."[7] Retailers know this and use sensuality more than any other way to sell their products. Sensuality is the perfect complement to successful materialism, even when a spokesperson and a product have little or nothing in common. We are led to think life will be better or happier or that we will have a more satisfying relationship or encounter if we can just obtain a certain product. Of course, this is false reasoning, but it is used time and again to sell products. Retailers know that sex sells, and within the marketing industry it is called "the concept." One philosopher stated, "Sex is the mysticism of materialism." Just look up the TV commercial "Never TOO Timeless." It illustrates perfectly how sensuality can sell a water faucet.[8]

Sensuality is a fleeting, subjective experience. It asks no questions and makes no judgments; yet it is not content until it succeeds in self-indulgence. Giving in to its allure results in opposition to God (2 Peter 2:10) and offers "acts of the flesh" (Galatians 5:19). Without prayer, our thoughts will naturally turn sensual (1 Corinthians 7:5). When we pray, our thoughts turn heavenward.

5. Greed. Materialism can turn even prayer into greed. Greed is the fuel that keeps pulling us back to material things. Jesus sets our possessions in the context of how we will stand before God when He points out the connection between greed and our possessions. "Then he said to them, 'Watch out! Be on your guard against all kinds of greed; life does not consist in an abundance of possessions' " (Luke 12:15). The rich man did not see his selfishness in building bigger barns (Luke 12:16–20). Jesus states the ultimate antidote in verse 31—seek the kingdom of God.

6. Narcissism. Materialism has the characteristics of a cult and is the perfect garden to grow narcissism; that is, becoming self-focused and egocentric. When allowed to flourish, narcissism will cunningly hide the truth while the image of selfishness is perfected. Possessions and wealth can make us think we are something we're not. Narcissism includes the personality traits of a fallen angel (2 Corinthians 11:14). In Isaiah 14:13, 14, Satan made five narcissistic statements:

> "I will ascend to the heavens;
> I will raise my throne
>   above the stars of God;
> I will sit enthroned on the mount of assembly,
>   on the utmost heights of Mount Zaphon.
> I will ascend above the tops of the clouds;
>   I will make myself like the Most High."

This kind of self-ambitious narcissism is the opposite of Paul's comment to "value others above yourselves" (Philippians 2:3–5). "If we empathize with other people to the point of merging our own identities with theirs, we care about them as much as we care about ourselves. Because we no longer place our interests above theirs, helping them is purely altruistic."[9] Moses showed altruism in his prayer. "But now, please forgive their sin—but if not, then blot me out of the book you have written" (Exodus 32:32). Later, Jesus demonstrated the ultimate altruism, and it led Him to the cross, where He died for us so that we could have a home in heaven.

7. Hoarding. Materialism is a progressive "religion" and ultimately leads to hoarding. The connection between the idea of ownership and possessions is more significant in this process than the number of possessions one owns. This problem is found almost everywhere in the world. A sense of ownership relates directly to identity, and a hoarder's identity is found in their possessions, which consume their life. We're not talking about the psychiatric disorder, but rather who or what we identity with—our possessions, or Christ?

16

Hoarding is an irrational perversion of management. It is the opposite of stewardship and the ultimate futility of the materialist's utopian dream, because possessions can rust and decay. "Love of self has led you to prefer earthly possessions even at the sacrifice of the heavenly. You choose the treasures that moth and rust corrupt rather than those which are as enduring as eternity."[10] We must blend our identity with Christ. Everything we live for is centered in Jesus. Paul stated clearly that Christ "is our life" (Colossians 3:4, KJV), and we are "alive to God in Christ Jesus" (Romans 6:11).

The antidote for materialism

Many would say that the antidote to the materialism described in this chapter is "giving." But even giving can be selfish. The giver and the gift can be corrupted. Givers can have wrong motives and give to the wrong cause.

The call of Elisha shows the opposite of what happened with the rich young ruler. Elisha left his wealth and in the end asked only for a double portion of Elijah's spirit (2 Kings 2:9–11). How can one have this kind of true unselfishness? The real antidote is obtained " 'not by might nor by power, but by my Spirit,' says the Lord Almighty" (Zechariah 4:6). "Might" refers to a big army, and "power" refers to a single warrior hero. The biggest army, the best books on psychology, or our closest family members cannot outweigh materialism's power over us. The strongest hero—a mentor, pastor, or spiritual guardian—is not strong enough to help us overcome materialism. The attraction of materialism is vanquished only by the Spirit of God. So simply turning to "giving" is not the antidote. We can only triumph over what this world has to offer when we allow God's Spirit to align our thoughts and actions with His loving and unselfish character.

---

1. Not his real name.
2. James A. Roberts, *Shiny Objects: Why We Spend Money We Don't Have in Search of Happiness We Can't Buy* (New York: HarperCollins, 2011), 87.
3. Ellen G. White, *Patriarchs and Prophets* (Mountain View, CA: Pacific Press', 1958), 161.
4. Alice Park, "Want to Live Longer? Turn Off Your TV," *Time*, Aug. 17, 2011,

http://healthland.time.com/2011/08/17/want-to-live-longer-try-turning-off-your-tv/.

5. Committee on Communications, "Children, Adolescents, and Advertising," *Pediatrics* 118, no. 6 (Dec. 2006): 2563.

6. White, *Patriarchs and Prophets*, 156.

7. Tim Kasser, *The High Price of Materialism* (Cambridge, MA: Bradford, 2002), 52.

8. "Never TOO Timeless: The Artifacts Faucet Collection," YouTube video, 0:35, posted by Nevs Model Agency, Mar. 19, 2015, https://www.youtube.com/watch?v=NyaFDpQ0EH4.

9. Adam Grant, *Give and Take: A Revolutionary Approach to Success* (New York: Viking, 2013), 222.

10. White, *Testimonies for the Church*, 3:250.

CHAPTER 2

I See, I Want, I Take

Karen stopped in front of the shoe store and scanned the window display. Her eyes caught the glitter of a pair of teal high-heel shoes. She let her breath out in a soft whistle. *They match my new dress perfectly*, she thought. *And they're on sale!* Karen knew that she was over her spending limit for the month, but the shoes might not be on sale—or even in stock—when she came back to town. She hurried inside the store and asked a clerk to let her try on a pair of the teal high heels in her size.

As she waited for the clerk to return, Karen thought of the credit card bill she had received the day before. She had spent several hundred dollars more than she remembered and knew that her husband wouldn't be happy about it. For a moment she considered leaving the store.

Before she could decide, the clerk arrived with the shoes. Karen slipped them on and stood up. *Perfect!* she thought. She asked the price, just to be sure the sign in the window was correct. It was.

"The sale ends tomorrow," the clerk said helpfully.

Karen didn't dare use the credit card, which was nearing its spending limit. She fumbled through the pockets in her purse, looking for money she might have tucked away and forgotten. Her hand brushed a small white envelope tucked in an inside pocket. Eagerly she pulled it out. Her heart sank as she realized it was the family's tithe.

Ugh! she thought, disappointed. *Why do we have to give so much to the church?* While her husband's job paid for the family's living expenses, her part-time job barely paid her personal bills. Karen looked again at the shoes. They fit as though they had been made for her. *The sale goes off tomorrow*, a voice in her head reminded her. *You deserve to look your best at church next week.*

Karen rose to her feet. "I'll take them!" she said quickly, before she could change her mind. She tore open the tithe envelope and removed the money. *God doesn't need it right now*, she rationalized. *Maybe I can work a few extra hours next week to repay this money.*

She accepted her package from the clerk and quickly walked out of the store before she could change her mind. Already the excitement of the new pair of shoes seemed to diminish.

Foundational oxymoron

Materialistic Christian—it is difficult to imagine how these two terms go together. No one would want that term applied to them. Yet a materialistic Christian can hide undetected in the church behind a disguise of humility. Regardless of the quantity of our possessions, we can give the impression that we are fine spiritually. This attitude is the greatest threat to the spiritual condition of the church. Is it possible that Christians in "good standing" can participate in "I see, I want, I take"?

An honest evaluation of the prosperity gospel reveals materialism at its core. This philosophy is simply that when I give, I expect something back from God. Paul warned Timothy (1 Timothy 6:5) against those who believed that godliness was a means to financial gain. At the heart of the prosperity gospel is the belief that words of Scripture can be used to force God to make His promises of health and wealth come true. This can be considered the religious side of materialism.

However, Jesus Himself did not dictate to His Father what to do for Him or attempt to trade His obedience for blessings. He asked and waited for the answer. He petitioned in submission. And so should we. Jesus didn't come to this earth to get rich but to give back. He was born poor, lived poor, and died poor. He turned down the riches of the world presented to Him in the wilderness by Satan (Matthew 4:8–10). Over the years, the prosperity gospel has strayed further from Scripture and increasingly "teaches that God blesses those God favors most with material wealth."[1] How do we combat the "I see, I want, I take" mentality that the prosperity gospel promotes? Here are four considerations.

Jesus

We start with Jesus. "The Son of Man did not come to be served, but to serve" (Mark 10:45). Serving as Jesus did is giving out of love without expecting anything in return. On earth Jesus "went around doing good" (Acts 10:38). He is not a means to wealth or poverty but the way to life eternal. We are not to love "the things in the world" (1 John 2:15, NKJV). To do so is hypocrisy—a perversion of the gospel. To avoid the trap of materialism, we are told, "Love the LORD your God with all your heart and with all your soul and with all your strength" (Deuteronomy 6:5). This is our privilege.

A materialistic Christian turns the walk of faith into grasping the broken handrails on a staircase that they think leads to heaven. It is futile. These handrails represent our attempts to buy our way into heaven with a quid pro quo from God. The "I see, I want, I take" mentality is a staircase to nowhere. It's as if we are unaware that our spiritual sensibilities are numbed by materialism. Trapped in this spiritual numbness, the rich young ruler traded his soul for his possessions. He did not recognize Jesus as the Son of God (Matthew 19:16–22; Mark 8:37).

Nowhere does Jesus say He will make His followers wealthy in this world. Instead, He promises that He will provide for our needs. In addition, Paul counsels that we should be content with the food and clothes God provides (1 Timothy 6:8). In the days of Paul, the Macedonians did not give to others in order to get rich (2 Corinthians 8:1–7). In the story of the good Samaritan, Jesus stressed giving unselfishly. It is not the amount of riches we have but what we do with what we have that measures a Christian's heart.

This is why the Sermon on the Mount (Matthew 5) is so important. "In the Sermon on the Mount He [Jesus] showed how its [the law of God's] requirements extend beyond the outward acts and take cognizance of the thoughts and intents of the heart."[2] These principles reveal a practical pathway to heaven that a Christian safely follows in a materialistic world. Simply put, we should pattern our lives after Jesus (John 5:30).

Emotion and reason

Stewards learn that wise decisions chart the course of their spiritual journey. They seek wisdom, knowing that "I want" usually ends in a bad decision. Wisdom is the result of the right use of reason and emotion—the two ingredients humans use to make decisions.

A person's ability to manage reason and emotion is called self-control. How does self-control work? Reason gathers information, and yet emotions dominate the process and become the driving force behind most of our decisions. Reason will even attempt to justify the emotional decision. Self-control is the process of keeping both reason and emotion serving the longer-term good rather than immediate gratification.

Most retailers sell their products by creating an emotional buying experience. Tapping into these emotions is considered entertainment. The experiences generated for the sake of prompting people to buy things only grow more sophisticated. Retailers know that most consumers are emotionally vulnerable, so they pressure them for an immediate decision. If given time to reason, we might not buy. Emotions disregard better judgment and influence us to buy on impulse what we don't need and probably can't afford. We take the path of least resistance and allow self-control to be set aside as we spend money we have not yet earned.

How can reason govern our emotions? Self-control is one of the gifts of the Spirit (Galatians 5:22, 23) that can be destroyed by materialism if we allow it. God wants us to use self-control for our own safety. He promises to help us in our weakness (Romans 8:26). The word translated as "self-discipline" in 2 Timothy 1:7 can also be translated as self-control. It is not punitive but freeing. It means acting out the will of God with a wise and sound mind. Developing the gift of self-control is becoming a master of the use of our will. Self-control must have direct influence over our emotions. Develop it when spending money. God promised, "I will instruct you and teach you . . . ; I will counsel you" (Psalm 32:8; see also Matthew 7:24; Isaiah 58:11).

The principles in Scripture are intended to set the course of our lives, while our emotions supply the motivation for action. If we stray from principles, emotions set our course and turn our desires into obsessions. If we allow our emotions to rule our lives, they will ruin our dedication and commitment to God. Jesus takes no pleasure in this. Says the wise man, "Commit your works to the Lord, and your thoughts will be established" (Proverbs 16:3, NKJV).

Spiritual eyesight

As I pulled up to my church one evening, I could see what appeared to be a homeless person trying to open the front door. Leaving the car lights on, I walked up to him and asked, "Are you OK?" I could see and smell that he was drunk.

As we stood at the door, he looked out toward my car and said, "Is that car moving toward us?" It wasn't, of course, but his intoxication confused his vision. Christians can be intoxicated with materialism, resulting in spiritual nearsightedness; wealthy and poor alike, we can see our closely held possessions, but we don't see Christ. We are deceived with materialism's promise of freedom and security, not realizing it can guarantee neither.

Christ Himself said, "It is easier for a camel to go through the eye of a needle than for someone who is rich to enter the kingdom of God" (Matthew 19:24). Materialistic Christians are tethered to their possessions, unaware of their spiritual condition. Like the rest of society, they tend to focus on the latest pleasure, comfort, or gadget, and they end up on a work-spend treadmill. Attachment to possessions reflects what we value in life, and these possessions provide false security. Piling up possessions is the greatest threat to God's people. He values *us*, not our possessions. God did not intend for us to worship possessions (Romans 1:25).

Israel forgot the Lord, and the nation's focus changed to the comfort of things (Deuteronomy 8:10–14). If we accumulate too much property and too many possessions, they make us drunk with greed. We make bad decisions with our blurred spiritual eyesight. Our faulty eyesight prevents us from seeing that God *will* supply all our needs (Philippians 4:19).

Selfish generosity

At least twenty-five Bible texts explain different aspects of generosity. But even generosity can be misdirected. While "I see, I want, I take" is the materialistic mantra, the materialistic Christian has also become skilled at selfish generosity, which is spiritualized covetousness. The one motivated by selfish generosity is looking for the gain from helping others, and they achieve it with cunning deception. "By covetousness they will exploit you with deceptive words" (Peter 2:3, NKJV). Even prophets were not immune (Jeremiah 6:13). Not even a rational conversation with a donkey could dissuade Balaam's greed for the king's gifts and the chance to make a profit (Jude 11). Selfish generosity is the pavement on the road to hell. It is the action of a fraud and represents one who believes their own lies.

The psalmist pleaded with God,

> Direct me in the path of your commands,
> for there I find delight.
> Turn my heart toward your statutes
> and not toward selfish gain.
> Turn my eyes away from worthless things;
> preserve my life according to your word (Psalm
> 119:35–37).

God is willing to "direct us, turn our hearts, and turn our eyes," a three-step process that can counteract our desire for material things. The first step is "direct us." God will guide and teach us as He did Adam and Eve, and we follow His direction. In some cases, that means removing ourselves from the temptation itself. The second step, "turn our hearts," expresses our permission to God to work in us and depend on Him to keep His principles, to block out our seeking selfish gain. The final step is "turn our eyes." This literally means to "make our eyes to pass." Looking at evil long enough makes it seem acceptable, but we give God permission to turn our eyes quickly and not let them linger on the things of this world. The world, on the other hand, tries to make all the things that are bad for us look enticing and things that are good for us look uninteresting.

Christians must not lose sight of Jesus in a materialistic world. He directs us and turns our heart and eyes through self-control, clear spiritual eyesight, and unselfish generosity as we counter the philosophy of "I see, I want, I take." We have the advantage in this battle because God is on our side. We may "approach God's throne of grace with confidence, so that we may receive mercy and find grace to help us in our time of need" (Hebrews 4:19).

---

1. Cathleen Falsani, "The Prosperity Gospel," *The Washington Post*, accessed May 15, 2017, http://www.washingtonpost.com/wp-srv/special/opinions/outlook/worst -ideas/prosperity-gospel.html.

2. Ellen G. White, *The Acts of the Apostles* (Mountain View, CA: Pacific Press, 1911), 505.

CHAPTER 3

God's Perspective

Mrs. Jenkins sat down at the desk of the tax preparer and laid a manila folder in front of her. The middle-aged man, named James, greeted her with a warm smile and opened the folder containing Mrs. Jenkins' tax papers. He quickly flipped through the income forms and calculated in his head that she had earned an income of about $30,000. Under these tax papers lay a thick pile of receipts that all appeared to be donations. A quick calculation indicated that Mrs. Jenkins had donated more than $12,000 to her church and charitable causes.

"Are you sure this is correct?" James the tax preparer asked, a puzzled look on his face.

"Oh, yes," Mrs. Jenkins answered. "I always give God what is His—and a good bit of what He's given me too. Are the donation receipts in order?"

"Well, yes," James reassured her. "But why—why so much?"

"James," Mrs. Jenkins answered as if she were speaking to her son, "I live by Philippians, chapter four, verse nineteen, which says, 'My God shall supply all your need.' He's given me a comfortable place to live and enough to pay my heating bill and buy my food. The rest I give back to Him."

"Are you saving any for a rainy day?" James asked her. "You know, for a new car, new furniture, medical bills?"

"Oh, I've saved some for doctor bills and such," she said with a sigh. "But I don't need a new car. My old one is running just fine. And I certainly don't need new furniture or new carpet at my age! I'd rather know my money is helping to change the world than wearing out under my feet! I don't plan to be in this old world a whole lot longer, and I want the money God has seen fit to give me to live on to make a difference in other people's lives."

James flipped through the remaining paperwork Mrs. Jenkins had organized for him. "Do you have any investments?" he asked.

"Just my pension plan," she replied. Then she stopped short. "I do have another investment plan," she answered.

"Do you have the correct investment income form for your taxes?" James asked.

"Oh, God doesn't send out income-tax forms," Mrs. Jenkins said, smiling. "This is God's investment fund. It's found in Matthew six, verses nineteen and twenty. I invest my funds where they won't rust or disappear in a stock-market crash or be siphoned away by hackers or thieves. It seems that the more I invest in God's bank, the more He gives me to live on. You should try it too!"

"Thank you, Mrs. Jenkins," James said. "I'll let you know when your paperwork is completed, and you can pick it up. It looks as though you'll receive a nice tax refund."

"Good!" Mrs. Jenkins said, pushing her chair back. "I've just agreed to help a young lady in India with her school bills! She wants to become a nurse. I just love it when God lets me have a part in deciding where to invest His funds." She smiled again as she opened the door to leave James's office. "Trust me. It works!"

God's perspective

Here we have a contrast between faith and materialism. Mrs. Jenkins has taken on God's perspective on material things, and she lives by His priorities. Many in the world are trapped in a very small view, asking questions that really say, "Have you saved up so you can save your yourself?" and "Why are you giving away instead of taking for yourself?"

What is God's perspective on possessions and how to view them? We will go through His foundational ideas. They provide us with the alternative to the failed views of the world.

Ownership

The foundation of materialism is the premise that we are owners. We go to great lengths to record our legal rights and prove our ownership of things. But the real owner of a house, for example, is typically the lender, not the one making payments or the one living in it. God, as Owner of all, describes His perspective and His relationship to our possessions on earth: "The earth is the LORD's, and all its fullness, the world and those who dwell therein" (Psalm 24:1, NKJV; see also 50:12). It is spiritually lethal for Christians to think they are owners of their possessions. Recognizing God as Owner is basic to understanding stewardship.

God's perspective on ownership is written in the Scriptures as statements of fact. From owning the cattle (Psalm 50:10) to the silver and gold (Haggai 2:8), everything in heaven and earth is His (1 Chronicles 29:11). A true owner acts at will and works for no one. Only God can make that claim. The hardest decision a steward must make is to accept that God is the Owner and we are the managers. "Indeed heaven and the highest heavens belong to the LORD your God, also the earth with all that is in it" (Deuteronomy 10:14, NKJV).

Just as we want to secure the property we have access to, so Jesus, who redeemed us, considers humanity His moral property. We are of such high value to Him that He wants to protect His investment. He "seals" us with His ownership (2 Corinthians 1:21, 22).

God holds the deed to this world as Creator and possesses legal ownership of us from sin through His redemption. He is entitled to an open relationship with His stewards, yet He does not force it upon us. That is why "we should regard ourselves as stewards of the Lord's property, and God as the supreme proprietor."[1]

At Creation, God entrusted the newly created world to Adam and Eve (Genesis 1:26–28). He did not give it to them to own, neither did He desire shared ownership. They were to manage God's possessions in perfect freedom. In the twenty-first century,

God has not changed this relationship. We have the responsibility to recognize our place in relation to God. He is the Owner and Redeemer of all. Even though we are created in His image, we are still *created* and not the Creator. God loves and cares for us as One who knows our every thought and human intricacy. His perspective toward us is only for good (Romans 8:28).

Creator

The ability to create something from nothing is an ability only God has. We do not have it. This defines who He is and gives Him a better perspective about the possessions of this world than we have (Hebrews 11:3).

God understands the working intricacies of how everything was created. This is a unique relationship that we are limited to. He gives life to matter; we cannot. He creates from the invisible; we cannot. He creates perfection; we create problems. Engineers and industries can design and mass-produce just about any product as long as they have the raw materials. But even when scientists say they have created matter in a vacuum, they concede it is from particles and antiparticles that already exist.

God's abilities cannot be explained or understood in human terms.

> The work of creation can never be explained by science. What science can explain the mystery of life?
>
> The theory that God did not create matter when He brought the world into existence is without foundation. In the formation of our world, God was not indebted to preexisting matter. On the contrary, all things, material or spiritual, stood up before the Lord Jehovah at His voice and were created for His own purpose."[2]

God-man

The title "Son of Man" appears eighty-eight times in the New Testament and has been called Jesus' favorite name for Himself. It identified Him with the human race. His humanity was the first step in closing the door to hell for believers, and His sacrifice on the cross and the resurrection permanently sealed it shut. Living an intense personal experience on earth as both fully God and fully man (1 Timothy 2:5) gave Christ a unique, authoritative perspective on human existence. He was tempted as we are, and thus identified with us, but He did not sin (Hebrews 4:15). No other human or "god" has ever accomplished this.

The blending of His divinity and humanity tells us what Jesus thinks of this world and especially humankind. "By coming to dwell with us, Jesus was to reveal God both to men and to angels. He was the Word of God,—God's thought made audible."[3] Jesus took a personal interest in us. How personal? "If we empathize with other people to the point of merging our own identities with theirs, we care about them as much as we care about ourselves. Because we no longer place our interest above theirs, helping them is purely altruistic."[4] Becoming human came at a huge personal cost of great humiliation for Christ, but He did so in order to be personally involved in rescuing us from sin. He holds a unique perspective on what it is like to be fully human and fully God.

If Christ had not become human, God would have been perceived as vindictive, unresponsive, and impersonal, hardly caring for His creatures. There would always have been confusion about who He truly is and whether He truly cares for us. To depersonalize God ultimately turns us against Him. The snake crafted his temptation into a seemingly benign theological discussion (Genesis 3:1–6) and won the argument with Eve. Satan blurred God's identity and His authority over her. This discussion continues today, with the theory of evolution painting a picture of God as an impersonal force in nature. This takes away the heart of the gospel.

Materialism depersonalizes God by replacing Him with things. In turn, we are depersonalized if we cling to our possessions. Recognizing Christ as the God-man teaches us to value His personal care for us and puts our possessions into the right perspective.

Redeemer

Jim Rohn, an entrepreneur, author, and motivational speaker, said, "You cannot change your destination overnight, but you can change your direction overnight."[5] If you are in financial debt, you can change your focus and direction immediately, and eventually work your way out of debt. Yet too many of us are comfortable living in debt, wondering why we are poor. Like the prodigal son, we do not have to continue toward our hopeless destination of being in debt to sin if we change our focus and direction.

Adam and Eve's decision to disobey God created a debt they could never pay back. Fortunately, God took responsibility for their debt. Essentially, He became the first mortgage holder. And since there is no such thing as outstanding debt in heaven, Christ, our Redeemer, paid it off. Christ's life, death, and resurrection were the price required to cover our debt of sin. He redeemed us from death. Now we can change our focus and direction. "Christ has paid the debt of sin for the whole world. In His great sacrifice, He embraces old and young. He endured the inconvenience of poverty, in order that He might bring to mankind the priceless riches of the heavenly home. He who was the Son of God, equal with His Father, He who made the worlds, has died to save every soul that will come to Him. How terrible it is for anyone to refuse to cooperate with Him, and to work against Him!"[6]

"None like Me"

"Keeping up with the Joneses" is an idiom we often hear, and we sometimes fall for this materialistic delusion. The children of Israel were told not to worry about their goods (Genesis 45:20), and neither should we. Material possessions are of little importance to God. He is not dependent on anything or anyone (2 Chronicles 20:6). Throughout the Bible we read stories of how God was forsaken for other gods (Jeremiah 2:11). In response He says, "Remember the former things, those of long ago; I am God, and there is no other; I am God, and there is none like me" (Isaiah 46:9). This is God's perspective in confronting competitors. He foresees the future and limits the power of His competitors (verse 10).

God's Perspective

One of the characteristics that makes God like none other is His involvement and relationship with His children, who live in a materialistic world. Throughout history, some Christians have been unprincipled, immoral, unworthy, and dishonest in the name of religion—the opposite of what Christianity should be.

No nation was so favored as Israel was, with God's visible interaction. "There is no one like the God of Jeshurun" (Deuteronmy 33:26). *Jeshurun* was a name for Israel and meant "upright." But Israel, though favored, was anything but upright. God is still the God of Jeshurun, and we are still anything but upright. Initially, no one seeks God out; instead, amazingly, God seeks us out.

On earth there was no one like Jesus. He was loved, worshiped, misunderstood, despised, and hated, but He simply states who He is:

"Thus says the LORD, the King of Israel,
And his Redeemer, the LORD of hosts:
'I am the First and I am the Last;
Besides Me there is no God' " (Isaiah 44:6, NKJV).

1. Ellen G. White, *Counsels on Stewardship* (Washington DC: Review and Herald®, 1940), 326.

2. White, *Testimonies for the Church*, 8:258, 259.

3. Ellen G. White, *The Desire of Ages* (Mountain View, CA: Pacific Press®, 1940), 19.

4. Grant, *Give and Take*, 222.

5. Jim Rohn, "You Cannot Change Your Destination Overnight, but You Can Change Your Direction Overnight," YouTube video, 0:59, posted by april thompson, October 18, 2016, https://www.youtube.com/watch?v=cl9ve2MoK88.

6. Ellen G. White, *Sermons and Talks* (Silver Spring, MD: Ellen G. White Estate, 1994), 2:300.

CHAPTER 4

Our Hope to Escape Materialism

Years ago during the Great Depression, a young pastor knocked at the door of a farmhouse in New South Wales, Australia. The farmer, Dave Oliver, opened the door and stared, surprised, at the visitor. Dave was sure this was the man he'd seen in a dream earlier in the week. He invited the pastor in.

The pastor offered Dave and his wife, Dora, Bible studies, and the couple agreed. Up till that moment the couple had not made church attendance part of their family's life.

While Dave and Dora accepted most Bible doctrines the pastor shared, Dave resisted when he learned about the Sabbath. Dave was convinced that if he left his farm to attend church, his large crop of watermelons—the family's main source of income at the time—would be lost to thieves or hungry neighbors.

Eventually, however, the Holy Spirit's promptings convinced Dave and Dora to trust God with their crops and worship God in church.

On Sabbath morning, while Dora helped the children prepare for church, Dave stood in his watermelon patch and committed his crop to God's care while the family was gone. And then he counted the watermelons—there were 456.

The family sat through church, but Dave didn't hear much of the pastor's message. He couldn't stop worrying about his melons.

As soon as church ended, Dave hustled his family into their horse-drawn wagon and headed toward home. Dora and the children sensed Dave's concern and sat in silence on the way home. When they arrived home, Dave told his son, Ted, to put the horse and wagon away while he headed to his watermelon patch. He didn't see any sign of theft. Methodically he counted his melons—467.

The next Sabbath the family again prepared to attend church. Once more Dave went to his melon patch, prayed for God's protection, and counted his melons. This time he counted 485. Then the family set out for church. This time Dave listened more carefully to the sermon; but as soon as church ended, he urged the family into the wagon and hurried home. Again Dave counted his melons. There were 493. Dave was convinced. He dropped to his knees in gratitude to God for protecting his melons—and convincing Dave that He would protect his crop while Dave and his family worshiped.

Dave and his family regularly attended church after that. Dave was known for his faithfulness and for raising the best fruits and vegetables in the area. Though relatively uneducated, Dave taught his children and grandchildren that God will meet them wherever they are and lead them where He wants them to be—as long as they are willing to follow.*

Experts tell us that to escape materialism we should watch less television, avoid window shopping, and de-clutter our lives. The main motivating factor behind this is the belief that the fewer material items people possess, the greater happiness they will obtain. But does this really achieve the desired goal of escaping materialism? Temporarily, perhaps. However, our focus on Christ—His character and His ways—is the most valuable reason for living, and that alone will determine whether we have lasting freedom and happiness. Here are some tools that will help us escape materialism's grasp.

---

* Originally published in a slightly different form in *Ordinary People— Faithful God*, ed. Nathan Brown (Warburton, VIC: Signs Publishing Company, 2007). Reprinted by permission of the author and the publisher.

Commitment

In this life, we have hope either in our possessions or in Christ. With hope in material things, we place our faith in earthly treasures that "moth and rust destroy" (Matthew 6:19, NKJV), and we try to be satisfied through selfish gratification. But that hope will turn to disappointment. Hope in Christ places our faith in a living, eternal Redeemer—where we will not find disappointment.

To strengthen hope and successfully find happiness in a materialistic world, we must commit to a relationship with Christ (Matthew 16:24). First we recognize a way of escape from the trappings of the world in the sacrifice of Jesus' death and His resurrection, and then we commit ourselves to it.

Commitment is not just a promise but a promise turned to action. It is not a one-time event but a continual devotion to Christ, with frequently renewed dedication to Him (Psalm 34:1). This commitment keeps our hope alive through the ups and downs of life. Renewing a commitment to Christ is part of the sanctification process.

The commitment to Jesus creates a much-needed relationship between the steward and the Owner. Stewards must discern between a conviction and a preference. Preferences are subject to change, but convictions are not (Daniel 1:8). The committed relationship does not waver or cease.

Jesus is the supreme Example of total commitment; He displayed it by His faithfulness to His Father. He said, "I do nothing on my own but speak just what the Father has taught me" (John 8:28). He glorified His Father on earth and finished the work He was sent to do (John 4:34).

In commitment, we figuratively cross a bridge and burn it behind us, never to turn back. When we desire to stay with Christ, He restores our dignity and raises it above the value of our possessions. He shapes noble principles in us. Our commitment to Christ is the only way we can break the cycle of materialistic thinking (Luke 18:22). We better ourselves by total commitment, not by making a few adjustments (Galatians 2:20).

Bible study

The Bible is mostly ignored, unread, and misunderstood by the world today. Studying it will draw us closer to God. It is the clearest form of communication He uses to reach us (Psalm 119:105). Materialistic values last a lifetime for most on this earth, but the application of biblical principles in one's life will last forever (Mark 13:31). Bible study elevates our character and helps us to focus on eternal truth instead of worldly possessions.

The Bible gives us hope through the promises of God. These promises have no time limitations (1 Peter 1:25), and they deal in moral and spiritual absolutes. What exercise is to the body, Bible study is to the mind! Careful study puts us ahead of others in understanding the realities of life.

Bible study teaches us mental discipline to make daily decisions and provides the principles to guide those decisions. Materialism, by contrast, is relative; in a materialistic, naturalistic world, everyone determines what is right or wrong according to their situation and preference. Materialism as a way of thinking is limited to this earth (1 John 2:17), and it nurtures pride and lessens our well-being. Pride is the pathway to destruction (Proverbs 16:18). But the humble will be exalted (Matthew 5:5, 6), Jesus told us. Materialism is "a bag with holes" (Haggai 1:6, NKJV), while Bible principles are living water in a leak-proof container.

"No other book is so potent to elevate the thoughts, to give vigor to the faculties, as the broad, ennobling truths of the Bible. If God's word were studied as it should be, men would have a breadth of mind, a nobility of character, and a stability of purpose, that is rarely seen in these times."[1]

A steward's prayer

Prayer is a ubiquitous practice in nearly all religions, but it is seldom understood. Prayer is not magic, meditation, or positive thinking. It remains a puzzle to science and a paradoxical discipline to psychology. To a materialist, prayer, even though it is addressed to a deity, is actually just mumbling to oneself. To a steward of God, prayer is a holy, persistent conversation with Christ (Luke 18:1) and a divine science that believers understand.

The discipline of prayer produces hope and power, while materialism mixes prayer with worldly desires. Materialism has no vocabulary for true prayer. It speaks in a shopping list of wants and takes the place of talking with God as with a friend. The term *materialistic prayer* describes an insistence that there is drinking water in an empty well. Empty wells are worthless and never satisfy. However, sincere prayer is to our spirituality as pure water is to our body.

Where there is true prayer, there is faith; where there is true faith, there will be prayer. Stewards understand and practice this to conquer life's challenges. "Prayer is heaven's ordained means of success in the conflict with sin and the development of Christian character. . . . The prayer of faith is the weapon by which we may successfully resist every assault of the enemy."[2]

The essence of prayer is being open to God (Ephesians 6:18). When we neglect prayer, we neglect faith, which is the perfect set-up for spiritual failure. But daily attention to prayer strengthens our connection with God and enables us to do what is right. "Jesus, when preparing for some great trial or some important work, would resort to the solitude of the mountains and spend the night in prayer to His Father. A night of prayer preceded the ordination of the apostles and the Sermon on the Mount, the transfiguration, the agony of the judgment hall and the cross, and the resurrection glory."[3] Jesus' prayers show an unbreakable relationship with His Father and illustrate how prayer overcame sin in Gethsemane (Luke 22:46).

Satan asserts that prayer is unnecessary, and if we listen to his lies, we will not exercise our faith. True faith and true prayer "are as two arms by which the human suppliant lays hold upon the power of Infinite Love."[4] When we pray, Jesus speaks to the Father on our behalf. Our prayers may be feeble, disorganized, or uneducated, but if they come from a sincere heart, Jesus pleads our case before His Father in the strongest terms possible.

Wisdom

Solomon accumulated a massive amount of possessions (1 Kings 10:26) and lived unrestrained in selfish pleasure. Why did he make one unwise decision after another? In following his own wisdom, he left God out of the equation. The wisdom of a steward is the result of spiritual and intellectual maturity. It is serving his master in humility. "Money, possessions, intellect, are but lent us to be held as a precious trust for the service of Christ. Reason, ability, knowledge, affection, property have been received from Jesus, and are to be used with wisdom to bring honor and glory to His name."[5]

Without Christ, wisdom is beyond our grasp. "Counsel and sound judgment are mine; I have insight, I have power" (Proverbs 8:14), says the voice of true wisdom. We could have all the wisdom in the world, but it is not enough to stand against what materialism offers unless we are faithfully connected to God.

Wisdom comes as a result of knowledge, understanding, and experience. Knowledge is information, and understanding comes from realizing and learning from the implications of the knowledge in situations (good or bad) I have experienced. The combination of these three give you wisdom. But it is more than that. "Humility, reverence, respect, adoration, faith—these are aspects of the wisdom that supersedes earthly knowledge. What is understanding? The answer is equally clear—'To depart from evil.' Understanding is more than intellectual—it is ethical. It demands a standard of living. Reverence and rectitude—these are the two great requirements of God. Micah (ch. 6:8) speaks of these two character traits as justice and mercy toward man and humility before God."[6]

The Holy Spirit

We often see a major clash between the desire for Christ and the desire for possessions (2 Kings 5:20–27). This can be a vague but intense struggle for Christian stewards. How can we keep from having possessions control our spiritual experience?

Material things are part of God's creation, and they have their proper place and value. Because of sin, we are trapped in placing too high a value on material things, and our escape from materialism depends on understanding and cooperating with the Holy Spirit. Materialism maintains control of us as long as it can use our senses to determine truth. But our senses can't be trusted to discern truth; that is the Holy Spirit's responsibility (John 16:13). Truth is absolute, but materialism tries to set up our possessions as absolute—a false theory. Our way of escape is to allow God "freehold ownership," meaning we become His property forever, and He is the Owner through the Holy Spirit. "It will only be by the incoming of the New Testament message of the Holy Spirit that Materialism will be overcome and prevented in future."[7]

The Holy Spirit guides the steward in the management of living a godly life. He is a protection for us against evil and corruption (2 Peter 1:3, 4). We tend to get comfortable in our lives and let our spirituality drift. This backsliding starts out subtle and unnoticeable, and it becomes like a spiritual cold. Then when our weakened spiritual condition is hit full force with the desire for this world, the allure of materialism becomes deadly to our souls (Exodus 32:1–6). We need the presence of the Holy Spirit to keep up our spiritual health as a defense against material desire.

This life is a battle of obedience to the world or obedience to the Spirit. True obedience is a matter of love, although we are constantly faced with hate, selfishness, and greed. Satan is the epitome of treachery (2 Corinthians 11:14) and rebellion toward God (1 Peter 5:8). He wants to draw us into his downward spiral of materialism. Stewards who choose God and faithfully serve Him have the provision of the Holy Spirit to guide them into a way of escape from anything this world has to offer (1 Corinthians 10:13).

---

1. Ellen G. White, *Christian Education* (Battle Creek, MI: International Tract Society, 1894), 119.

2. Ellen G. White, *Prayer* (Nampa, ID: Pacific Press®, 2002), 52, 62.

3. Ibid., 173.

4. Ellen G. White, *Gospel Workers* (Washington, DC: Review and Herald®, 1948), 259.

5. Ellen G. White, "Unselfish Service, No. 1," *Pacific Union Recorder*, July 14, 1904, par. 7.

6. Francis D. Nichol, ed. *The Seventh-day Adventist Bible Commentary* (Washington, DC: Review and Herald, 1954), 3:573.

7. W. H. Griffith Thomas, *The Holy Spirit of God* (Eugene, OR: Wipf and Stock, 2001), 3.

CHAPTER 5

Stewards Reinstated

A wealthy man died leaving no heirs. Following the man's instructions, his lawyer arranged to sell the man's estate. The estate included valuable artworks and furnishings. On the appointed day, hundreds of people thronged the estate hoping to buy the man's goods at a fraction of their value.

The auctioneer began bidding with a portrait of the dead man's son, who had preceded him in death. But those gathered were not interested in the portrait, which was not painted by a renowned artist and held no great value in their eyes. "Who will start the bidding on this portrait?" the auctioneer asked. No one responded. "Who will give me $10?" Still there was no response. Someone in the audience urged the auctioneer to move on to the truly valuable objects in the estate, but the auctioneer insisted on selling the portrait first. Frustrated mutters filled the room as those gathered waited to get to the real prizes.

A woman dressed in plain clothes stood and offered to buy the painting for $10. That sum was, to her, a great deal of money. The auctioneer noted her bid and asked, "We have $10! Who will give $20?" When no other bids were made, the auctioneer shouted, "Going once! Going Twice! Sold to the woman on my left for $10."

As the auctioneer continued with the sale, the woman paid the cashier and received her portrait. She returned to her small home and looked lovingly at the portrait. She had once been the boy's nanny and had loved him deeply. The picture would hang in her humble home, a sweet reminder of the boy she had loved who had died far too young.

As she examined the painting, she noticed a slight bulge between the canvas and the paper backing. Carefully she slit the backing and found an envelope marked "Last will and testament." Surprised and somewhat confused, she took the paper to the estate's lawyer for examination. The lawyer read it through with a look of astonishment on his face. Then he laid it in front of him and looked at the woman who had brought it. "Madam, this is indeed the last will of the estate owner. Can you tell me how you came to have it?"

"I went to the auction hoping to find some small reminder of the little boy I had cared for. I loved him so and could not bear for his portrait to be discarded. I found this envelope hidden under the backing of that portrait."

"According to this will," the attorney touched the paper before him, "the person who purchased the portrait of his son inherits the estate of the father. Madam, your love for the boy and your faithfulness to him has been richly rewarded."

Job description

At the beginning of this world we were created as stewards to manage it and be accountable to God. God did not give Adam and Eve the specific name of steward, but the responsibilities and status He gave them defined that role. The stewardship of the garden was our job, so to speak, in the order of creation established by the Creator. For the human race, being a steward is innate and just as much a part of our DNA as our eye color and height. We will always be stewards.

After the fall of Adam and Eve, many things changed, but they were still to be stewards. The question was, for whom? For God or—floundering on our own—for Satan?

Understanding the identity of a steward is key in our relationship and responsibility to God. Ever since sin came, God has been calling us back to our rightful position and responsibility.

Stewards Reinstated

He wants to reinstate us as His stewards. This is no small task, but it is God's way of teaching us who we are, by what we do. We must learn what it means to be reinstated stewards.

Above all else, being God's steward in a world of sin begins with accepting the Redeemer. We are "entrusted with the gospel" (1 Thessalonians 2:4), to care for and manage it. Every Christian's vocation is to manage the gospel. This is our most important responsibility and requires great dedication. Some have to relearn thought patterns and discover new perspectives. In an imperfect world, our living and preaching the gospel is the core of a steward's heart and life.

Stewards in the Bible

In the Old Testament a steward is a manager who knows and depends on the owner. The word *steward* first occurs in the story of Abraham's servant Eliezer of Damascus (Genesis 15:2). Joseph is called a *steward* or overseer (Genesis 39:4), as is Arza, steward of King Elah (1 Kings 16:9, NKJV). These references have no spiritual application, direct or implied. They simply define what the steward does.

The New Testament continues this Old Testament concept but adds a spiritual aspect. Humanity is entrusted with the "mysteries of God" (1 Corinthians 4:1, 2). Spiritual leaders are given the responsibility of "[managing] God's household" (Titus 1:7) and are "stewards of the manifold grace of God" (1 Peter 4:10, NKJV). This puts the responsibility of a steward on a higher plane than managing possessions, although it does not exclude that task.

As a steward you have two responsibilities. The first is to manage the possessions God gives you. If you can't manage your possessions, "who will trust you with true riches?" (Luke 16:11; see James 2:5). The second is to manage the spiritual riches that come from God. "Faith and love are the true riches, the pure gold which the True Witness counsels the lukewarm to buy."[1]

Reinstated identity

What does a reinstated steward look like? As a reinstated steward, you understand who you are in relationship with the Owner. You are restored to the position of manager under your Director. In an orchestra, the second violin follows the first. In the business world, you are leading from the second chair with your boss as first chair. The second chair's leadership is limited and always stays within the vision of the first chair (the boss). And of course, relating to the Boss is the key to getting it right. "The right relationship is everything!"[2] A godly steward depends on the relationship that she or he has cultivated with the Owner (Daniel 6:10).

Coming home from a trip one time, I left the baggage claim area of the airport and proceeded to the curbside waiting area where my wife, Jan, was to pick me up. When her car pulled up, I opened the door and saw Stewardship Jack, our black labradoodle, was squealing with delight, wagging his tail so wildly that it went thump, thump, thump, thump against the car interior. He knew who I was and would have been in my lap if there had been enough room for a 65-pound dog and a six-foot-tall man in the front seat. Jan and I are Jack's world. We travel, work, and have friends, and though Jack is dependent on us, he has his own personality. Animals know their owner. But all too often, humans don't (Isaiah 1:3). In Christ, we have a reinstated identity as His stewards.

Tangible possessions

Reinstated stewards must understand how to manage tangible possessions. We are restored to the responsibility established in the Garden of Eden. "God gave our first parents the responsibility of subduing the earth, governing the animal kingdom, and caring for the Garden of Eden (Gen. 1:28; 2:15). All this was theirs not only to enjoy, but to manage."[3]

Most of us are not farmers and ranchers, but we are managers of God's possessions. Possessions are mostly tied to wealth, and although there is nothing inherently wrong with them, they have the capability to separate our hearts from God. We love to see, hold, touch, buy, sell, and feel these objects. Their physical existence offers security and satisfaction, and we therefore give them our admiration. We may feel that we own them, but this is the wisdom of the world. It is self-conceited thinking in light of God's instructions for us to manage our possessions and not think of them as ours alone (Luke 12:22). "When God gives someone wealth and possessions, and the ability to enjoy them, to accept their lot and be happy in their toil—this is a gift of God" (Ecclesiastes 5:19).

The true value of our possessions is based on the Owner's perception of them, and we have the responsibility to manage that which He owns. This is difficult to practice because God is invisible and our possessions are very much visible. In reality, we are managing the wealth of God (Psalm 24:1).

God has reinstated us to properly manage tangible possessions that will build His character in us. Such character development is worth more than all the possessions we have (1 Peter 1:7). However, God is not opposed to wealth. Abraham was rich and had many possessions, and he was also called a righteous man (Genesis 15:6). "The ruler's possessions were entrusted to him that he might prove himself a faithful steward; he was to dispense these goods for the blessing of those in need. So God now entrusts men with means, with talents and opportunities, that they may be His agents in helping the poor and the suffering. He who uses his entrusted gifts as God designs becomes a co-worker with the Saviour. He wins souls to Christ, because he is a representative of His character."[4]

Intangible possessions

Like tangible possessions, intangible ones must be managed well. God values very highly the intangible possessions He has given us. The Bible is a tangible possession, but it contains intangible spiritual possessions from God (1 Peter 4:10). We must manage these riches just as we would tangible ones. These possessions nurture the soul and are used in spiritual growth.

We do not own the intangible possessions God provides for us. Yet we can have confidence that they are ours. He gave them to us as an assurance of victory over sin.

Redemption is intangible and, through faith, our most valuable possession. It helps us keep perspective in our stewardship of other possessions. We are to take hold of the gift of redemption (Romans 6:23; 1 Timothy 6:12). In contrast, materialism cannot offer or comprehend eternal life. "Only in the light that shines from Calvary can nature's teaching be read aright. Through the story of Bethlehem and the cross let it be shown how good is to conquer evil, and how every blessing that comes to us is a gift of redemption."[5]

Redemption is ours because Jesus paid the ultimate price. "In Him we have redemption through His blood, the forgiveness of sins, according to the riches of His grace" (Ephesians 1:7, NKJV). "We have" means redemption is ours; it is not borrowed or loaned, but is ours today. This is why the "helmet of salvation" (Ephesians 6:17) and the whole armor of God is so vital in protecting our possession of redemption. "He keeps what He has redeemed, redemption is among our possessions; He has given it to us, and He preserves it to us."[6]

"We have" (Hebrews 6:19) a hope that is an anchor. "We have" (1 Corinthians 2:12) the Spirit so we can understand what God has given to us. We are responsible for our actions (Numbers 32:23). Before we accepted Christ we did not have these possessions, but God has now entrusted us with them.

Transformation

We go through a transformation, and we see the results. Christ gave instructions to His stewards to go and make disciples. His disciples are to follow and learn. His stewards are to manage a righteous life.

One might ask the question, Are you a disciple or a steward? "Show me a steward and I will show you a disciple. Show me a disciple and I am not confident you will always find a steward. Discipleship and stewardship are not always synonymous terms."[7] While the terms overlap each other, they are different. Only God's stewards are managers of the grace entrusted to them.

Christ has revealed to His stewards all He possibly can about what He is like. We must take all that He has shown us and manage our lives well as we grow in Him, blameless (Titus 1:7) "as faithful stewards of God's grace in its various forms" (1 Peter 4:10).

Stewards Reinstated

Christians have not always been good stewards of the message of salvation in Christ. Religious persecution, injustice, and wars have all been committed in His name. We should not partake in that spirit. When our responsibility is rightly understood, we will practice it now, and we will spend eternity studying this mystery of love.

---

1. White, *Testimonies for the Church*, 4:88.
2. Mike Bonem and Roger Patterson, *Leading From the Second Chair* (San Francisco: Josey-Bass, 2005), 34.
3. Ministerial Association, *Seventh-day Adventists Believe* . . . (Silver Spring, MD: General Conference of Seventh-day Adventists, 2005), 27.
4. White, *The Desire of Ages*, 523.
5. Ellen G. White, *Education* (Mountain View, CA: Pacific Press˚, 1952), 101.
6. Francis William Bourdillon, *Our Possessions: A Short and Simple View of Some of Those Good Things Which Are the Present Portion of the Believer* (London: J. Nisbet, 1904), 15.
7. Patrick G. McLaughlin, *Haggai & Friends* (printed by author, 2010), 20.

CHAPTER 6

The Steward's Brand

Years ago a farmer was looking for a hired hand to help him on his farm. A quiet young man named Frank answered the farmer's ad and offered to work for him. "What kind of experience do you have?" the farmer asked. Frank answered simply, "I can sleep when the wind blows."

The farmer was puzzled by Frank's comment and almost turned him away. But as he studied the young man's calloused hands and well-muscled arms, he decided to give him a chance. "Well," said the farmer, "I don't know what that means, but I'm going to hire you anyway." The farmer and Frank worked side by side in the fields, sowing crops, building fences, and caring for the farm animals. The young man worked hard, but he said little.

And then one night the farmer was awakened by howling winds and tree branches clapping against the house. He leaped out of bed and ran to the barn to check on the animals. There he found the doors securely locked, the windows closed, and the animals safely in their stalls. Outside he found the haystacks staked down.

As the farmer fought the wind on his way back to the house, he repeated Frank's strange statement, "I can sleep when the wind blows." Suddenly he realized what Frank had meant. The young

51

man had done his job carefully and thoroughly, even before he knew that a storm was coming. He had been a faithful steward.

Brands are extremely important to sellers. They promote recognition and motivation and are built up over an extended period of time. Retailers create their brands to distinguish themselves from other products. Do stewards have a brand?

God's brand is love (1 John 4:8, 16), and He invites us to join His brand. "By this everyone will know that you are my disciples, if you love one another" (John 13:35). If we accept God's brand in our lives, it will be revealed to others by how we live. Love as a brand is a nuance of the character of Christ and stands out compared to the world's ideals. Faithfulness is the baseline from which loyalty, a clear conscience, obedience, and accountability spring. Trustworthiness is a bookend to these moral traits. These show love.

Faithfulness

The starting point for a steward in managing God's possessions is faithfulness. "Moreover it is required in stewards that one be found faithful" (1 Corinthians 4:2, NKJV). Why? Because "God is faithful" (1 Corinthians 1:9) and "[His] faithfulness endures to all generations" (Psalm 119:90, NKJV; also see Deuteronomy 7:9). Being faithful is the clearest and one of the most challenging characteristics of God's brand to follow. It is a significant, basic key in being a steward. Yet for many, being faithful is short-lived. Too often we start with good intentions but don't follow through. To be faithful or unfaithful stems from the many decisions we make, built over time. The harder we fight in the spiritual battle of faith, the simpler the decision will be. Faithfulness is required and represents the baseline that guides us in serving Christ.

Even though some of the individuals mentioned in Hebrews 11 went through spiritual failures, they are still known for their faith. Writers single out Abraham as the "father" of the faithful (Galatians 3:7), pointing to him as the ultimate example of faithfulness. Through his triumphs and failures, "he was called God's friend" (James 2:23). Being faithful is a virtue and is a step beyond belief that will find public expression. "Bible religion, practiced, will make you kind, thoughtful, faithful."[1] Faithfulness is showing you believe in God through your actions. This is part of the steward's brand. "You can prove yourself elected of Christ by being faithful; you can prove yourself the chosen of Christ by abiding in the vine."[2]

Loyalty

Loyalty is a rare commodity. "Without loyalty there can be no love. Without loyalty there can be no family. Without loyalty there can be no friendship. Without loyalty there can be no commitment to community or country. And without those things, there can be no society."[3] Traded loyalty is a divided loyalty and will destroy faithfulness, but faithfulness expresses loyalty.

Hachiko, an Akita, has been called Japan's most loyal dog. His story is told in the movie *Hachi: A Dog's Tale* (2009). Every day he returned to Tokyo's Shibuya train station to wait for his master, who never returned. Loyalty is part of an animal's DNA. We could learn some things about our loyalty to God from the animals He created.

Clear conscience

Faithfulness is the foundation of a clear conscience. When past failures accuse us of sin, the faithful steward understands "the forgiveness of sins" (Matthew 26:28). A forgiven Peter, though he had sinned by denying Jesus three times, had a clear conscience when he later said to the crippled man, "In the name of Jesus Christ of Nazareth, rise up and walk" (Acts 3:6, NKJV). A clear conscience refines the steward's brand and reveals a mature faith.

To have a clear conscience one must have a good conscience (1 Timothy 1:5), or an educated conscience. It is "without offense toward God" (Acts 24:16, NKJV). It lives and acts according to how it has been educated. When educated from Scripture, it does not fear accountability.

For years Joseph's brothers lived with offended consciences for selling him to the Ishmaelites. It was not until after Jacob's death when they realized that Joseph forgave them that their consciences fell silent (Genesis 50:19–21). Faithfulness ensures a clear conscience as it is tested by our actions. "We are to remember that we are not pieces of inanimate mechanism, but intelligent beings, able to choose the right and refuse the wrong, with a clear conscience and a pure purpose."[4] Our only solution is to allow Christ to cleanse our consciences "from dead works to serve the living God" (Hebrews 9:14, NKJV).

Obedience

"By faith Abraham . . . obeyed" (Hebrews 11:8). Paul said, "Lord, what do you want me to do?" (Acts 9:6, NKJV). Jesus was willingly obedient to His Father throughout His earthly life (Philippians 2:8; Hebrews 5:8). He made obedience practical in His actions, and He taught obedience to others through His parables. His life was the supreme example of obedience "to the point of death, even the death of the cross" (Philippians 2:8, NKJV).

True faithfulness will prompt a consistent outflow of obedience, not a compliant relationship. Compliance is obeying the speed limit when monitored by a traffic officer but ignoring it once you pass him or her. Compliance is because you have to; obedience, freely given. Faithfulness enjoys obedience. It is a matter of love that ventures into the unknown. "A missionary society wrote to David Livingstone deep in the heart of Africa and asked: 'Have you found a good road to where you are? If so, we want to know how to send other men to help you.' Livingstone wrote back: 'If you have men who will only come if they know there is a good road, I don't want them. I want men who will come if there is no road at all.' "[5] Being faithful to God will drive one to do what seems impossible. Faith bears the weight of obedience.

Accountability

Accountability is a simple way to measure your successes and failures. It is an obligation that love accepts because it reveals what we have done. Accountability gives us freedom. Without it, stewards will experience an atrophy of love that becomes political and judgmental.

Stewards understand that they are accountable to God (Romans 14:11). God's accountability has three parts: First, God keeps a record of our lives. He numbers the hairs on our head (Matthew 10:30), numbers and names the stars (Psalm 147:4), knows our every word (Matthew 12:36), and knows those who fear Him (Malachi 3:16). Second, we are responsible to God for our actions (Ecclesiastes 12:14; Galatians 6:4, 5). This reveals our true character. "I must know that the grace of God is in my own heart; that my own life is in accordance with his will; that I am walking in his footsteps. Then my words will be true, my actions will be right."[6] And third, our participation is required (Romans 14:12). Individual accountability will be destroyed if any of these three characteristics are missing.

Trustworthiness

Once I sat on a plane next to an off-duty airline pilot. We were talking about a pilot's skill in flying these incredible machines, when he commented, "We only promise to get you down." After a second longer pause, I said, "Thank you very much, I appreciate that." Is an airline pilot trustworthy? Yes. However, the pilot can't 100 percent promise you a safe landing. Knowing this risk, we trust the pilot and fly anyway. Is Jesus trustworthy? "Jesus Christ is the same yesterday and today and forever" (Hebrews 13:8). Is Lucifer trustworthy? "For he is a liar and the father of lies" (John 8:44). Are we trustworthy? We may say, "I love God," but our actions reveal that truth. Trustworthiness is what people recognize in us when our talk matches our walk (see 2 Kings 22:7). We are truthful, not agents of espionage. Trustworthiness is a by-product of our faithfulness.

Being faithful gives those who observe us the opportunity to decide whether we are trustworthy or not. When I was sixteen, I attended boarding school and worked in the maintenance department to help pay for my tuition. One hot summer day, my job was to cover the repaired pipes with dirt. The dirt was hard—as if it had been baked in an oven—but finally the large hole was filled, and the ground was landscaped.

A few days later, while waiting for the maintenance work assignment, I overheard the maintenance man say to a school administrator, "If I give John a job to do, I know it will get done.

He is trustworthy." I have never forgotten that comment, and it comes to mind when I am faced with difficult tasks. For me, no is not an option; I must do my work to the best of my ability.

When trustworthiness is actualized in our lives, others will see it. It is what they think of us. Their observation is the result of our faithfulness, loyalty, clear conscience, obedience, and accountability. For God to call us trustworthy is amazing. This trait is the result of having a dependable and reliable relationship with Him. He knows that if we clothe ourselves with this trait, we will live by His principles, and we can be trusted with what He has given us to do. Trustworthiness is a moral purpose that has no position or ulterior strategy. "Whoever can be trusted with very little can also be trusted with much" (Luke 16:10).

So what is *your* brand? Do others consider you trustworthy? If the steward's brand is based on love, then what flows out from us will deliver a righteous reputation that is faithful, obedient, accountable, and trustworthy.

1. White, *Testimonies for the Church*, 6:171.
2. Ellen G. White, *Our High Calling* (Washington, DC: Review and Herald®, 1961), 77.
3. Eric Felten, *Loyalty: The Vexing Virtue* (New York: Simon and Schuster, 2011), 3.
4. Ellen G. White, *That I May Know Him* (Washington, DC: Review and Herald®, 1964), 290.
5. Dan Miller, *48 Days to the Work You Love* (Nashville: B & H, 2005), 108.
6. Ellen G. White, "Address to Ministers," *Review and Herald*, May 30, 1871.

CHAPTER 7

Honesty With God

A few years ago a neighbor told me how God had blessed them when they were called to serve as a missionary overseas. They had decided to rent out their home while they were gone and prayerfully chose a young couple to rent to. The husband was a student at the nearby university, and the wife worked full time to support the family. The missionary couple were not naïve; they knew that families can be hard on their home, so they decided on a rental amount that would help cover the cost of replacing carpets, painting, and repairing any damage that occurred during their absence. When they returned home after five years, they were stunned to find their home in near-perfect condition. The young couple had made several repairs that were needed during their absence and had even cleaned the carpets and repainted the rooms that needed it. The missionaries decided to give the young couple more than their expected deposit back. "You have been wonderful stewards of our home," the wife said when she called the couple with the news. "If you want a reference, please let me know!"

But not all renters are as faithful as this young couple. Another missionary couple who lived nearby returned to their home to find that the couple who had rented their home had left behind more than empty rooms. The carpets were spotted with greasy stains, and the house was full of bugs. The refrigerator was moldy, and the dishwasher wasn't working. The couple spent weeks and hundreds of dollars cleaning out trash, replacing carpets, and repainting walls. They even found a hole in the wall behind a hastily moved dresser! "And these people were church members," they sighed wearily. "They had promised to care for our home while we were gone in exchange for a reduced rent. But we lost money—and confidence—in their honesty."

Although postmodern culture considers total honesty to be a vague, irrelevant ethic, honesty is a virtue to be prized. All biblical principles fail without honesty. Honesty with God is one of the most misunderstood biblical principles, and one that stirs negative emotions and controversy. Even some theologians seem to think this practice is not necessary. However, the high moral standard of honesty is personified in Christ. He said, "I am the way, the truth, and the life" (John 14:6, NKJV). For many, honesty with God is the first thing they think of when stewardship is mentioned.

Rightly understood, tithing is the quintessential activity of a steward's honesty with God. Being honest with tithe is an outward expression of one's theology and a spiritual action that—when done with the right motive—destroys legalism. To fully incorporate the trait of honesty with God into our characters, we must understand the dynamics of what an honest tithe is. It must be a conviction of the heart for us to follow God's will.

A matter of simple honesty

God is honest, fair, and straightforward. Never has He been dishonest, nor will He ever be. However, dishonesty is never far away from us in this sinful world. Since we are sinners, our honesty runs on a spectrum that ranges from simple honesty to half-truths to white lies and all the way over to outright dishonesty.

Christ's parable of the sower describes the seed that falls on good soil as representing those of "honest and good heart" (Luke 8:15, KJV), signifying a foundation of our spirituality that is essential to stewardship. As money is the currency in the economy, so our honesty is the currency of our spirituality.

Honesty keeps open our access to divine power. Dishonesty,

on the other hand, is pride acting out. When we are dishonest in small things, we find it easier to be dishonest in larger matters. God hates dishonesty (Proverbs 6:16, 17).

Honesty is not valued by many people, and even religion is not indicative of one's being truly honest. Researchers in psychology have discovered the "honesty-humility" personality trait, and they say it "matters in many aspects of people's lives. It underlies their approaches toward money, power, and sex. . . . It orients them toward certain attitudes about society, politics, and religion. It [even] influences their choice of friends and spouse."[1] We are born with the honesty trait, but it must be educated. Properly formed in us with biblical principles, honesty becomes our guide (Proverbs 11:3).

"Try Me now"

For anyone who has not returned tithe, it can seem like a difficult step to take, at least to start with. But God says, "Try Me now" (Malachi 3:10, NKJV). This means we will act to see whether what God promises is true. He has already accepted the burden of proof by asking us to try Him.

Some are fearful (Psalm 56:3) that 90 percent of their income will not go as far as 100 percent and they won't be able to manage. Others say tithing is not required but rather more of a suggestion. They may say it isn't necessary today, or they can't afford to do it. But ignorance, disregard, or excuses to not "try" are not sufficient reasons for us to deny returning what God says belongs to Him.

The ultimate meaning of "try Me now" is that it proves God's existence. To see the proof, we must have two components—a good argument and a valid demonstration of evidence—or the proof fails. The argument is that the tithe belongs to God and the demonstration of "trying God" by returning it will give evidence that He keeps His promise of blessings to us. It is more than just a legal transaction or a valuable way to get blessings, as wonderful as they are. The evidence God gives will prove the argument.

When we "try" God in this visible way, we are making a personal statement to others that God exists and we trust that His plan works. If the principle of tithing had never been required, those who argue against it might have a case. But God has required it from the beginning, and He has not changed His commandment. Attempting to get out of God's directive to "try Me" is faulty logic (Psalm 14:1) and denies that God is who He is by replacing His directive with our limited understanding.

"Unselfishness, the principle of God's kingdom, is the principle that Satan hates; its very existence he denies. From the beginning of the great controversy he has endeavored to prove God's principles of action to be selfish, and he deals in the same way with all who serve Him. To disprove Satan's claim is the work of Christ and of all who bear His name."[2] In our tithing, Christ is working through us to dispel selfishness.

A statement of faith

Once, after I finished giving a Bible study to a man on tithe, he said, "If God will pay all my bills, then I will pay a tithe. We don't need to study anymore." On another occasion a person told me that they were no longer going to support the "rebels" with their tithe. To treat tithing this way is hypocrisy. Returning the tithe is a statement of faith in God. It is a personal testimony and a statement of conscience that shows up in the core of our belief system. Rejecting a faith requirement of God is rejecting His character and His expectations of obedience. We cannot claim His name and at the same time reject His claims on us.

Jacob did not miss this concept. After he saw a vision of a ladder into heaven, he made this vow: "If God will be with me, and keep me in this way that I am going, and give me bread to eat and clothing to put on, so that I come back to my father's house in peace, then the LORD shall be my God. And this stone which I have set as a pillar shall be God's house, and of all that You give me I will surely give a tenth to You" (Genesis 28:20–22, NKJV).

Our participation in tithing is a covenant of faith, an agreement between God and His people. Such a covenant is described as having a "command/promise structure."[3] This structure is found in Malachi 3:10. It contains the command to "bring the whole tithe" and the promise that God will "open the floodgates and pour out so much blessing." This covenant is designed to draw us to God and affirm His presence and gifts. Returning tithe shows our faith in one of God's clear promises. He will not disappoint, "For no matter how many promises God has made, they are 'Yes' in Christ" (2 Corinthians 1:20).

Holy to the Lord

Tithing was practiced and considered sacred in ancient civilizations. In Babylon "we find Tiglath Pileser, Nebuchadnezzar, Nabonidus, Belshazzar, Cyrus, and other sovereigns, with all classes of the people in the Euphrates valley, as well as Phoenician colonists in Carthage—all of them annually offering a tenth of their increase."[4] The Greeks considered a tenth of their cropland was "sacred to Diana."[5] Among the Romans, "Hercules is the god most frequently mentioned among them as the receiver of tithes."[6] Even Festus, the ruler who listened to Paul's testimony (Acts 25), "is reported as saying that the ancient Romans offered every sort of tithe to their gods."[7]

The Bible gives two essential theological facts about the tithe: it "belongs to the LORD; [and] it is holy to the LORD" (Leviticus 27:30). "He has reserved it to himself to be employed for religious purposes. It is holy. Nothing less than this has he accepted in any dispensation. A neglect or postponement of this duty, will provoke the divine displeasure."[8] We return our tithe to a living, holy God. This is a sacred act.

Honest revival, reformation, and tithing

When I was a little boy, my dad said, "Johnny, did you see the man I baptized today?"

"Yes," I replied, wanting more food on my plate.

"At the top of the baptismal tank he turned and said, 'Hey preacher, the water didn't hurt my money,' and turning around, he showed me his money. 'Why did you bring your money into the baptistry?' I asked as he stood holding the money. 'I wanted my money converted,' he said. Johnny, never forget, your money must be converted."

That is about the clearest illustration of revival and

reformation I know. Christ is at the center of both. Revival without reformation makes a lukewarm Christian, and reformation without revival leads to legalism. The man that my dad baptized wanted to be revived *and* reformed in his whole life, with no part of it left out. What I find fascinating is that there is no need for a lack in tithe funds for supporting gospel workers. The lack comes from followers of Jesus not making the statement of faith. There is a need for revival and reformation. "If all professed Christians would faithfully bring their tithes to God, his treasury would be full."[9]

Being honest with God is liberating. Dishonesty is a burden. Don't turn into a burden what God has designed to be a blessing. We are called to be honest, to try God, to be faithful, and most of all to be holy—pure, without any blemish. "For it is written: 'Be holy, because I am holy' " (1 Peter 1:16). God makes holy those He saves. Those He saves will recognize that tithe is sacred and holy, to be used in His work.

1. Kibeom Lee and Michael C. Ashton, *The H Factor of Personality* (Waterloo, ON: Wilfrid Laurier University Press, 2012), 4.

2. White, *Education*, 154.

3. Ronald E. Vallet, *The Steward Living in Covenant* (Grand Rapids, MI: William B. Eerdmans, 2001), 50, 51.

4. Henry Lansdell, *The Sacred Tenth; or, Studies in Tithe-Giving, Ancient and Modern*, vol. 1 (London: Society for Promoting Christian Knowledge, 1906), 20.

5. Ibid., 26.

6. Ibid., 29.

7. Ibid., 33.

8. Ellen G. White, "Will a Man Rob God?" *Review and Herald*, May 16, 1882.

9. Ibid.

CHAPTER 8

The Impact of Tithing

Eva quickened her steps as she left the university student center and returned to her small apartment. It had started to sprinkle, and if the predicted rain arrived before she got home, her feet would be soaked. She wished she could afford to buy a pair of shoes to replace the ones with holes in the soles.

"Please, Lord, hold back the rain till I get home," she whispered as she ran. When she arrived home, she placed her shoes near the door with a prayer of thanks to God for holding back the rain.

The next day as Eva prepared for school, her roommate, Alicia, pointed to her shoes near the door and said, "Why don't you throw away those old shoes and get a new pair?"

"I will when I get paid," Eva answered quietly.

"You can't afford a pair of shoes, but you give money to your church?" Alicia asked accusingly. "Don't you think God would understand if you spent some of that money on shoes? The church has more money than you do. They don't care that your shoes have holes in them."

Eva didn't reply, but she had to admit to herself that sometimes she had been tempted to withhold her tithes and offerings—just until she could catch up on her bills. But she was determined not to take God's money to meet her needs, no matter what Alicia—or anyone else—said.

Eva faced another problem. Her final semester of university was coming, and she would be doing her student teaching at a local high school. There was no way she could both work and teach that semester. How could she pay her tuition and fees in order to graduate? Eva turned to God with her dilemma, and He gave her peace and a promise to supply all her needs.

Together we fund the mission

People give to political campaigns because they are interested in either promoting the ideology of their candidate or blocking the rival. Many contributors don't join in the campaigning, but their money indicates what they believe in and support. In the same way, God's people make a statement about what they believe in when they contribute to His work. What is the impact of returning 10 percent of one's increase to God?

Jesus said, "Go into all the world and preach the gospel to all creation" (Mark 16:15). Tithe is a global responsibility and helps keep our focus on God's mission. "Voluntary offerings and the tithe constitute the revenue of the gospel."[1]

In many situations, the amount of money available seems to determine what can or can't be done. It's as though we settle for "little money, little impact; lots of money, lots of impact."

The likelihood that an initiative will be accomplished depends on members working together to financially fund the mission. It creates a stronger work, clearer identity, and a greater chance of success.

More people can be reached if we are united rather than fragmented (1 Corinthians 12:12; 2 Corinthians 11:7–9). Without financial and mission unity, we may tend to fund our own agendas and priorities rather than give to the greater cause. Funding God's mission does not function in isolation. A local church cannot accomplish a world mission. It takes all the members who believe in the world mission to fund it.

Tithe as a system is the greatest source of funding and the most equitable method for carrying out God's mission. However, mission cannot move forward with confidence when most

Christians do not return tithe. "Only 9.4 percent of all [US] Christians . . . give 10 percent or more of their incomes."[2] Furthermore, the more people earn, the less they give,[3] and "more than 70 percent of congregational income is spent on local operations."[4] In order for the church to achieve its mission, the system of financial provision for the mission must be clearly connected in the minds of members.

The best ways to fund the mission are through encouraging and urging systematic giving and through increasing the number of givers. Increasing the number of faithful tithers is not an easy task because of the ingrained culture of the church and the influence of materialism. The Seventh-day Adventist Church (or any charitable organization) cannot sustain an adequate long-term mission if fewer and fewer members are giving more and more of the dollars.

To reverse this trend, we must first give ourselves completely to God (Romans 12:1, 2). We must be fully converted! Second, members must be taught "that a portion of their income belongs to God and is to be sacredly bestowed to His work."[5] As strange as it may seem, this requires a conversion of our money! Third, pastors must set the example and practice tithing.[6] Fourth, we must refrain from redirecting the tithe: "Let none feel at liberty to retain their tithe, to use according to their own judgment."[7] God has a right to tell us where to bring the tithe, and He instructs that it be brought into the "storehouse," that is, the church. Fifth, members in the twenty-first century must internalize systematic generosity. It was called systematic benevolence in the 1850s. "If systematic benevolence were universally adopted according to God's plan, and the tithing system carried out as faithfully by the wealthy as it is by the poorer classes, there would be no need of repeated and urgent calls for means at our large religious gatherings. There has been a neglect in the churches of keeping up the plan of systematic benevolence, and the result has been an impoverished treasury and a backslidden church."[8]

Blessings beyond comprehension

A few days before Eva's final semester began, she was summoned to the office of the university's financial assistance advisor. Eva nervously entered the man's office.

"Good morning, Eva," the advisor said as he motioned her to a chair and took his seat. "I see that you've been on our work-study program for three years." She nodded and added how much she had appreciated the work.

"We've had a large number of students applying for the work-study program this year," he said. "More students have applied than we have funds to help." Eva's heart sank. *God,* she thought, *I'm so close to finishing school. Please open the windows of heaven for me now.*

The financial advisor looked at Eva and smiled. "We've looked at your financial situation and your grades, and we'd like to ask you to give up your work-study benefits. In its place, we will give you a scholarship to complete your remaining semester. Are you willing to do that?"

Eva sucked in her breath. "I would get paid for *not* working?" she asked. He nodded and offered her the paperwork and asked her to sign it. She signed the papers and then stood and whispered, "God has answered my prayer today!"

Eva left the advisor's office thanking God for encouraging her to seek first His kingdom and showing her just a part of the "all things" He was adding to her life.

If tithing results in blessings, as Malachi 3:10 says, why aren't more people participating? What blessings from God have they have not claimed? People seem to see only a divine abstract that has not become concrete reality for them. Blessings beyond comprehension start with the promise of eternal life. We may try, but it is humanly impossible to grasp the full meaning of the promise. However, there are blessings in this life that we can comprehend very well.

Blessed means being found in God's favor. A blessing of tithing is a deepened spiritual maturity. The practice of returning tithe increases faith that leads to the blessing of inner peace. For this reason, returning a faithful tithe affects the spiritual health of one's soul. When we do not tithe, we rob God, but we also rob ourselves of His blessings and fail to experience a deeper faith.

God's blessings reflect His perspective toward us (Jeremiah 29:11), and this can be seen only through the eyes of faithful, obedient stewards. The blessings are spiritually experienced and spiritually discerned.

Tithing makes no sense unless we have a relationship with Jesus. He is the more-than-adequate reason we take up the practice. As Jesus gave His life to bless us, we are to bless others. In tithing, we are able to be a blessing to others. "Blessing is not one-dimensional, as in the accumulation of material assets. Someone saying, 'I have been blessed with a big house or car,' is acknowledging only one dimension of it. But blessing is not one-sided where we are just the recipients of it."[9]

Purpose of the tithe

The purpose of the tithe, is to say that the tithe is unequivocally connected to mission. Pastors are to advance God's mission. We might say that evangelism is their business. The ultimate purpose of the tithe is to bring people to a saving relationship with Christ.

This is most clearly seen when people are baptized into the body of Christ. Which is more important, the pastor or the mission? Those new converts and their decisions to follow Jesus represent the mission of the church and the greater purpose of the tithe. The closer we tie souls for the kingdom to the purpose of tithe, the greater the impact on the tither and the world. The gospel worker is privileged to participate in "the most important work ever given to men, the work of bringing the last message of mercy before all nations, kindreds, tongues, and people. The Lord's treasury must have a surplus to sustain the work of the gospel in 'regions beyond.' "[10]

The storehouse

Seventh-day Adventists consider the storehouse to be the local conference or mission, where tithe distribution takes place to support the world work and local pastors. "The tithe is the Lord's, it is his interest money, and it is to be paid regularly and promptly into his treasury."[11] The conference is not a bank for deposits but functions as a "pass-through account." A percentage of the funds from the storehouse is used to support each of the following: local pastors, the local conference, the union conference, the division, and the General Conference mission.

However, we may have overlooked a more meaningful reason for a storehouse. Your heart will always follow where you put your money. As the old gospel song states, "This world is not my home, I'm just a-passing through. My treasures are laid up somewhere beyond the blue." The real storehouse is in heaven.

"Those who really feel an interest in the cause of God, and are willing to venture something for its advancement, will find it a sure and safe investment. Some will have a hundredfold in this life, and in the world to come life everlasting. But all will not receive their hundredfold in this life, because they cannot bear it. If entrusted with much, they would become unwise stewards. The Lord withholds it for their good; but their treasure in heaven will be secure. How much better is such an investment as this!"[12]

Today's tree of knowledge of good and evil

Among the ancient Egyptians, tithing took various forms, and "the god's portion was deemed sacred; and . . . to diminish it was regarded as a sin."[13] Where did the tithe concept start? "Tithe was a Babylonian institution."[14] The Romans date its start to Romulus and Remus. Greeks date it to the Trojan war. However, historians have found "no secular inscription—not even in the code of Hammurabi, . . .—that tells us when or where tithe-paying began, or who issued the law for its observance."[15]

In Eden, Adam and Eve did not tithe, but the spiritual significance and meaning of the tithing principle originated there. Jesus taught it to Adam by explaining why he should not eat of one tree (Genesis 2:16, 17). "This tree God reserved as a constant reminder of His ownership of all. Thus He gave them opportunity to demonstrate their faith and trust in Him by their perfect obedience to His requirements."[16] This was a simple test for Adam and Eve. No great hardship or exertion was required as proof of loyalty to God. They were to avoid eating of the tree of knowledge, which would show that they recognized Him as Owner of all.

The same principle applies today when we return the tithe. God has given us the simple test of tithing that is equal to the test of the tree in Eden. Failure to tithe results in a slow asphyxiation of the soul. Refusing to return tithe is a sin, the equivalent of taking the fruit of the tree of knowledge. By our willingness to tithe we pass the faith test that eluded our first parents and receive the blessing they longed for.

1. Ellen G. White, "A Warning Against Hypocrisy," *Review and Herald*, Feb. 2, 1911.

2. Christian Smith and Michael O. Emerson, *Passing the Plate: Why American Christians Don't Give Away More Money* (New York: Oxford University Press, 2008), 37.

3. Ibid, 44.

4. Ibid, 52.

5. White, *Testimonies for the Church*, 9:246.

6. Ibid.

7. Ibid., 247.

8. Ibid., 3:409.

9. Kerry Kirkwood, *The Power of Blessing* (Shippensburg, PA: Destiny Image, 2010), 21.

10. White, *Testimonies for the Church*, 6:286.

11. Ellen G. White, "How Much Owest Thou?" *Signs of the Times*, Jan. 13, 1890.

12. White, *Counsels on Stewardship*, 232, 233.

13. Lansdell, *The Sacred Tenth*, 19.

14. Ibid., 14.

15. Ibid., 38.

16. White, *Testimonies for the Church*, 6:386.

CHAPTER 9

Giving Offerings

God had been good to Elizabeth's family, there was no doubt about it. While they weren't rich, they had proven God's invitation to test Him, and He had never failed. Whenever the family had a specific need, they asked God, and He had stepped in and supplied their need. Even when Elizabeth's husband, Don, lost his job, God had provided. After much prayer, Don decided to start a new business. Though money was still tight, the new business began to grow.

The family saved wherever they could, and Elizabeth became adept at finding what they absolutely needed at the best prices. Eventually her two children needed new clothes, and Elizabeth dreaded a trip to the mall. She explained to the children that she had only a limited amount of money to spend on clothes. As was her practice, she asked God to help them find what they needed at a price they could afford.

As Elizabeth and the children walked through the mall, her daughter pointed to an upscale store and asked to go in. Elizabeth's heart sank. This shop was popular but out of their price range. Then her daughter said, "Look, Mom! A sale!" Elizabeth decided to go in but reminded the children of the budget they had to stick to.

As the three entered the store, a salesperson greeted them and offered each of them a scratch-off card that would give them a percentage off their purchases. They scratched the cards and found that two of the cards offered 25 percent off, but the third one offered 75 percent off everything in the store—even the sale and clearance items! Elizabeth gasped. Perhaps they could afford a few items of clothing after all.

Elizabeth and her children walked through the clothing departments selecting what they needed most. Instead of a couple of cheap T-shirts, the children were able to buy good-quality clothes for 75 percent off the sticker price—even the sale prices! Elizabeth was even able to get some clothes for her husband and a few for herself—all within their budget.

As they paid for the clothes, the salesclerk congratulated them on getting the biggest discount card offered. Elizabeth thanked the clerk, but in her heart she knew that it was no accident that they had received that card. They had asked God to supply their needs, and He had—and so much more.

God loves to give. It's part of His nature, and He does it freely. He invented the idea that "it is more blessed to give than to receive" (Acts 20:35). Jesus' sacrifice on the cross and the grace that His death provided are the best presents we have been given.

In fact, giving is a "philosophy of life and relationship which is wrapped up and illustrated by the example of a little girl who had been given 10 new pennies. She held them all in her hand, admiringly. Then she took one and laid it aside.

" 'This,' she said, 'is for Jesus.' She took a second and said, 'This is for you, Mummy.' A third, 'This is for you, Daddy.' And on to the tenth. 'And this is for Jesus.'

"Her mother said, 'You forgot, dear; you have already given one to Jesus.'

" 'I know,' she replied, 'but that belonged to Him; this is a present.' "[1]

God desires that we make this gift of the Spirit (Romans 12:8) an automatic expression of gratitude. Giving reflects His character in our life. However, some Christians don't give, or if they do, they give very little. They don't think about the consequences.

Grace—the ultimate gift

Without Christ, grace is a hopelessly abstract idea. But with Christ, it is the ultimate, most complex and wonderful gift ever given to humanity. Grace is divine mercy—the most valuable gift that God has for us. "For by grace you have been saved through faith, and that not of yourselves; it is the gift of God, not of works, lest anyone should boast" (Ephesians 2:8, 9, NKJV). Its power reaches down to the bottom rung of human perversion and the deepest humanistic thought. God gave His grace to the world whether people wanted it or not. We may reject it, but we cannot stop it, delay it, or change it. Grace stands alone, waiting for us (Revelation 3:20), and it is activated only if we accept it.

There is no selfishness in grace. Where grace is needed, selfishness is present; but where grace is accepted, selfishness is rejected. "It is good for our hearts to be strengthened by grace" (Hebrews 13:9). It cuts through hate and selfishness so that they may be completely cut away.

The grace of God includes His deepest thoughts and emotions toward sinful humanity (Psalm 139:17). We are of such worth to God, and He has such love for us, that He gave all He had to keep us. "Divine benevolence was stirred to its unfathomable depths; it was impossible for God to give more."[2] We are His treasure; His heart is focused on humanity.

Grace satisfies our soul by replacing our filthy garments with white robes of righteousness (Revelation 7:13, 14). When we accept it, we become givers of grace. Without accepting the gift of grace, we will be motivated to make few sincere offerings of gratitude.

Our best offering

Our best offering to God is ourselves, "a living sacrifice" (Romans 12:1). Strange as it may seem, we are the most valuable asset we have to give. This is true only because of what Jesus has done for us. By giving ourselves, we put God first with our best offering. Mary understood this when she offered her best to Jesus (Matthew 26:7, 12). In the twenty-first century, the bottle of perfume she bought might be worth about US$44,000. She knew the sacrifice that Jesus would soon make. Those who love much give much, and those who love little give little.

When we give an offering, we are giving back to God what is His in the first place (1 Chronicles 29:14). He accepts it from a heart filled with gratitude (2 Corinthians 9:7).

Motive for giving

As a young pastor, my inexperience got me into more than one sticky situation. I remember two wealthy men in my church, George (not his real name), who was not a church member but never failed to attend on Sabbath, and the other, Sam (also not his name), an older man who was recently baptized. At a church work bee, some of the deacons wanted me to talk to George because they didn't like what he was doing. I immediately jumped in and expressed what the deacons wanted me to say. George responded, "If that is the way they want to do it, I quit." Throwing down the tools, he got into his car and left.

Sam bought an organ for the church, without notice. Some of the leaders asked me to tell Sam such things needed board approval beforehand. Again, in my inexperience, I repeated to Sam what the board members had said. As he stood listening to me explain the board's position, tears welled up in his eyes and he said in a shaky voice, "Pastor, I am sorry. I didn't mean any harm. I just wanted to do something for my church."

The motive for giving, whether in time, money, or objects, is one of the most frequent internal spiritual struggles that a Christian goes through. Actions will reveal the motives of our heart.

Jesus watched a poor widow put two coins into the collection box at the temple. He told His disciples, "She out of her poverty put in all that she had, her whole livelihood" (Mark 12:44, NKJV). "This poor widow has put in more than all" (Luke 21:3, NKJV). Jesus recognized an astonishing display of character, while her motive was hidden from those around her. To give everything you own is a radical faith experience that reflects total commitment.

God alone weighs our motives in giving (Proverbs 16:2; 2 Corinthians 8:12). "The eye of God takes cognizance of every farthing devoted to His cause and of the willingness or reluctance of the giver. The motive in giving is also chronicled."[3]

Loving God for what He has done for us (1 John 4:19) is the only true motive for giving (1 Corinthians 13:3). A young man gives his fiancée a dozen roses because they are sweethearts. He is motivated from love. "Love of money" (1 Timothy 6:10) and love of the world (1 John 2:15) are the motivations that try to keep us from giving to God. But true love, "the basis of all true benefi-cence, is more frequently and more emphatically enjoined than any other Christian duty . . . [Matthew 22:37–40]. Here we have a concise and comprehensive summary of the whole duty of Christian benevolence"[4]

The poor

Jesus said, "The poor you will always have with you" (Matthew 26:11). They are to be faithful stewards too. The Old Testament says that the poor were allowed to freely glean the fields at harvest time (Ruth 2:3). But the concept of the poor in Scripture is much broader than just those in need of food or money.

Christ left the riches of heaven and became poor so we might become rich (2 Corinthians 8:9). He considered the poor a spe-cial group that He singled out for attention during His earthly ministry. Two things occur when we help this special class. First, giving to those who are poor transfers wealth from earth to heaven (Mark 10:21). "Every opportunity to help a brother in need, or to aid the cause of God in the spread of the truth, is a pearl that you can send beforehand, and deposit in the bank of heaven for safe keeping."[5]

Second, and far more important, is that when we help those who are poor, it is as if we are doing it for God Himself (Matthew 25:40). Helping the poor is like lending money to God in that He becomes a debtor who "will pay back what he has been given" (Proverbs 19:17, NKJV; Ecclesiastes 11:1). You keep for eternity only what you have given away by doing good.

Cheerful giver

How can you be "a cheerful giver" (2 Corinthians 9:7)? Three steps: gratitude leads to generosity, and generosity leads to cheer-fulness. Here are two metaphors as we "taste and see that the LORD is good; blessed is the man who trusts in Him!" (Psalm 34:8, NKJV):

1. Tasting God is having a personal experience with Him. He encourages us to experiment with expectations and venture into a close experience with Him (Psalm 145:9). Tasting God is a liv-ing relationship based on the certainty of God's goodness regard-less of the situation (Romans 8:28), and it will be revealed through our countenance (Proverbs 15:13).

2. Seeing God by faith makes clear for us the reality of what we have experienced. It is like our response when turning on a light in a dark room.

Cheerfulness is the product of tasting, seeing, and feeling gen-erosity. "So let each one give . . . , not grudgingly or of necessity; for God loves a cheerful giver" (2 Corinthians 9:7, NKJV). The word *hilaros*, translated "cheerful," actually means hilarious, so we are talking about hilarious giving.

"Experience is knowledge derived from experiment. Experi-mental religion is what is needed now. 'Taste and see that the Lord is good.' Some—yes, a large number—have a theoretical knowledge of religious truth, but have never felt the renewing power of divine grace upon their own hearts."[6] God invites us to do good as He has done good (Psalm 119:68; 3 John 11). He promises that we will not be disappointed. As Jesus gave His life for us and keeps providing daily for our needs, He desires that we give back to Him and to humankind and taste the results.

---

1. Carlyle B. Haynes, *The Legion of the Tenth* (Nashville: Southern Publishing Association, 1956), introduction.

2. White, *Testimonies for the Church*, 9:59, 60.

3. Ibid., 2:519.

4. J. Ashworth, *Christian Stewardship*, 4th ed., 29.

5. Ellen G. White, *Christian Service* (Hagerstown, MD: Review and Herald, 2002), 221.

6. White, *Testimonies for the Church*, 5:221.

CHAPTER 10

The Role of Stewardship

Mitch had taken a job in a major corporation and was learning his way around his new department. He joined the other employees for lunch so he could get to know his fellow workers. Most of the employees, he noticed, were friendly and enjoyed chatting with one another during breaks—and often much longer. Mitch liked the camaraderie of his new department and quickly fit in.

He noticed that one man, Frank, was different. Frank was friendly and helpful, but when the lunch hour ended, Frank was back at his desk working. He rarely stopped to talk to someone unless it was about business, and if something detained Frank during the day, he would stay late to make up the time.

Mitch was curious about Frank. As the two walked out of the building one day, Mitch asked, "What is it with you, Frank? I notice you don't hang around the lunch room after one P.M., and you're always at your desk working. You must really love your job!"

Frank smiled at Mitch and answered, "I do enjoy my work, Mitch. But my loyalty isn't to this company. It's to God. And He demands accountability. Taking office time to chat or do something personal is stealing. This company pays me to do a specific job, and if I spend some of my work hours on personal things—even chatting with a friend—I become a thief."

Mitch was quiet for a moment. "That's kind of hard to swallow," he responded. "Everyone chats with others during the day. It keeps up morale and helps us do our job better. Don't you think the boss understands that and expects it?"

"Yes, I guess so. But that doesn't make it right. Being an honest worker is part of being a good steward. And that's what God expects of those who belong to Him."

Mitch thought for a few moments. "I hadn't thought about that," he said. "I'm a Christian. I return my tithe and give offerings, but I thought that was all God required."

"Actually," Frank said, "God tells us exactly what He expects of His followers. It's found in Micah 6:8. He says, 'What does the LORD require of you but to do justly, to love mercy, and to walk humbly with your God?' [NKJV]. As I understand it, that means that in every part of my life, God expects me to be His steward, managing my time, my money, my heart, so that everything I do and say and think honors Him."

"Frank, I think you're onto something there," Mitch said. "I'm going to start praying that God will make Micah 6:8 real in my life. Thanks for your advice. And hey, your life reflects what you've just told me."

Stewards are accountable to someone. They are either wise stewards like Joseph, who served Potiphar (Genesis 39:4–6), or unwise like the dishonest steward in Christ's parable (Luke 16:1–13). For this reason, stewardship plays a vital role in the Christian's life.

We can understand the significance and role of stewardship by studying the parts of a chariot wheel, much like the wheels of the temple carts in 1 Kings 7:33, as they relate to our experience with Christ and the walk of faith. First we must identify God as the wheelwright, the person who makes a wooden wheel. The wheelwright has been called an artisan because making a wheel requires great precision. He or she must combine the skills of carpentry and the knowledge of a blacksmith. The math skills and craftsmanship of the wheelwright are the greatest factors in determining the quality and durability of the wheel.

Axle: Christ as the center

The live axle of our wheel is Christ. A live axle is the shaft on which the wheel rotates and also the mechanism that transmits power to the wheels. As it is central to the motion of the wheel, so is Christ central to our progress. We cannot move without His power. The axle keeps the wheels in position, just as Jesus keeps us in position when we become attached to Him. The live axle also carries the weight of the vehicle, just as Christ carries the weight of salvation, making our burden light (Matthew 11:28–30). "Let us bear in mind that Christ is the great central heart from which the life-blood flows to every part of the great body of humanity."[1] Christ is the center of the steward and the stewardship that carries the weight of our actions, just as a live axle provides stability, allowing the wheels to rotate and carry the chariot forward.

Christ is at the center of our wheel. He is the anchor for our conduct. "And let us run with perseverance the race marked out for us, fixing our eyes on Jesus, the pioneer and perfecter of faith" (Hebrews 12:1, 2). He is the living, powerful Christ, and only through Him are we able to succeed in any practical application of our theology. "Fixing our eyes on Jesus" makes Him the center of our life. His influence affects everything we think and do. He is the core identity for our earthly purpose and eternal security. If Christ is not our center, we are not His stewards, and any attempt at stewardship is futile.

Hub: Sanctuary doctrine

Once, while I was in the middle of giving a Bible study on the sanctuary doctrine, a listener asked, "What difference does this teaching make anyway?" I forget the exact answer I gave her, but I never forgot her question. The difference that the sanctuary doctrine makes can be illustrated by the wheel hub.

The hub holds the wheel onto the axle. The hub (also called the nave) of a chariot wheel is made of elm because its grain does not easily split when spokes are inserted. For the wheel to turn in a balanced way, it must be made "true," which means the hub must be in the exact center of the wheel. When spokes are inserted, they can be tightened or loosened in a process called dishing, which sets the hub to center. The hub is crucial in holding the wheel onto the axle. It must be strong, stable, and precisely made for the axle and hub to fit and work together.

The wheel hub illustrates the sanctuary doctrine by which we study the Bible and apply it to life. This biblical doctrine is the cornerstone for Seventh-day Adventists (see Daniel 8:14; Hebrews 8:1–5). No single text can encompass all aspects of it. This doctrine provides a unique lens through which we look at all of our other biblical beliefs. When we understand the importance of Christ in the sanctuary, acting as our judge and advocate, we can see why our Christian belief system is unique. It provides the moral guidance that is reflected in an awakened conscience of the steward. Anchored in this truth, the steward can distinguish truth from error. Understanding the centrality of the sanctuary in our theology is what guides us in "rightly dividing the word of truth" (2 Timothy 2:15, NKJV). Theology affects practical living, our stewardship. Right doctrine will effect right living and is crucial for stewardship to have a redemptive outcome.

The sanctuary doctrine "opened to view a complete system of truth, connected and harmonious, showing that God's hand had directed the great advent movement and revealing present duty as it brought to light the position and work of His people."[2] "It is the base of a coordinated system of truth."[3] This is "the basic hermeneutical framework for the development of a unique doctrinal system."[4]

Spokes: Christ-centered doctrinal beliefs

The first wheels invented were solid, heavy circles of wood. Spokes were invented to make the wheel lighter and the chariot faster. The spokes act as wheel braces and are carefully made by the wheelwright so as to perfectly fit when inserted into the hub. They cannot be loose or be driven in too tight, for this would lessen the strength of the wheel. As we said, this process of inserting the spokes is what makes a "true," or balanced, wheel.

The wheel spokes represent the different doctrines (2 Timothy 3:16, NKJV; Titus 1:9) and beliefs[5] that Christians hold. They reveal what is important to us and govern our behavior. Beliefs can be changed or distorted, as we see in the life of King Saul (1 Samuel 13). A belief you are willing to change is a preference that accommodates your whims, depending on the situation. It has no moral standard and is out of "true." Beliefs we will not change are solid convictions that give us moral absolutes (Acts 9:1–22) to live by. The spokes of doctrines and beliefs must be anchored in Christ and influenced by His ministry in the sanctuary, and they must be tested for biblical truth (Isaiah 8:20). Every generation struggles looking for truth, but when the system is in place, "then you will know the truth, and the truth will set you free" (John 8:32). This system has a huge impact on your stewardship.

Rim: The three angels' mission

The wheelwright next attaches an outer rim of wood, called the felly, around the spokes that have been trimmed to make a perfect circle. The felly is made of several pieces of wood that must fit tightly onto the spokes.

The rim represents the three angels' messages for our mission. While the broad concept of the three angels' messages includes everything we stand for as Seventh-day Adventists and is therefore part of the hermeneutical framework illustrated by the hub, the mission of Revelation 14:6–12 is the action that keeps us rolling, as the rim of a wheel does. It keeps us from becoming static and inward focused, so that we lose the reason and purpose that the Seventh-day Adventist Church exists.

When the three angels' messages for mission surround our system of doctrines (the spokes) that are based on a biblical understanding of the sanctuary doctrine and that is focused on Christ, we gain a unique worldview, designed for God's people who are living at this point in earth's history. "The three angels of Revelation 14 represent the people who accept the light of God's messages and go forth as His agents to sound the warning throughout the length and breadth of the earth. Christ declares to His followers: 'Ye are the light of the world.' "[6]

Band of iron: Stewardship

The final step on the chariot wheel is the installation of the "tire."

An iron band was superheated, forged, hammered into place, and then cooled with water. As the iron contracted, it forced the joints of the wheel to tighten. This tight fit made the wheel last longer, since it would not be constantly jarred and loosened as it came in contact with the ground. There were no glue or nails in the wheel, so the iron rim is all that held the wheel joinery together.

This tire, represents stewardship. We are all stewards who make contact with the world in every kind of situation. Our stewardship holds everything else in place. It is how we manage situations based on our Christian religion. "Theology seeks to think out the meaning of . . . [the] encounter [with God]. Stewardship seeks to live it out."[7] Our unique worldview sets the stage for us to make theology pragmatic and practical, where we manage tangible and intangible possessions for God's glory. This leads to accountability to the Wheelwright who put it all together. Stewardship is the moment of truth in how we apply what we believe to our life. This makes every contact with life an extension of our beliefs.

A band of iron properly set illustrates practical sanctification. It is how our daily activities relate to our salvation experience. This harmony is a daily conversion of life, demonstrating "that he who began a good work in you will carry it on to completion until the day of Christ Jesus" (Philippians 1:6). "Every living Christian will advance daily in the divine life. As he advances toward perfection, he experiences a conversion to God every day; and this conversion is not completed until he attains to perfection of Christian character."[8]

The night Peter denied Christ three times was the night a grieving Peter's stewardship was reset. After Christ ascended to heaven, Peter stood before those who had heard him curse, and he spoke fearlessly of Jesus. Peter had been converted anew. His values were realigned. The iron band on his life had been set tight and true. Likewise, our Spirit-led actions continually realign us with our biblical doctrines and with the truth of Jesus. This is not a theological exercise of ideas but a daily living out the will of God (Romans 12:2; Psalm 84:11).

Our greatest challenge

At every point that the stewardship tire makes contact with the ground, we are faced with the responsibility of understanding and skillfully executing successful management. God is truth (John 14:6), but what money claims is a half-truth. The greatest challenge a steward will encounter is the relationship to and the proper management of the life God has provided. Our unique worldview illustrated by the chariot wheel will help keep us from certain ruin.

---

1. Ellen G. White, "Duty to the Poor, the Erring, and the Wandering," *Review and Herald*, Oct. 16, 1894.

2. Ellen G. White, *The Great Controversy* (Mountain View, CA: Pacific Press`, 1950), 423.

3. LeRoy Edwin Froom, *Movement of Destiny* (Washington, DC: Review and Herald*, 1971), 87.

4. Alberto R. Timm, "Seventh-day Adventist Eschatology, 1844-2001: A Brief Historical Overview," 287.

5. As in the 28 fundamental beliefs.

6. White, *Testimonies for the Church*, 5:455, 456.

7. T. A. Kantonen, *A Theology for Christian Stewardship* (Philadelphia: Fortress Press, 1956), 6.

8. Ellen G. White, *My Life Today* (Washington, DC: Review and Herald*, 1952), 249.

CHAPTER 11

Debt—A Daily Decision

Greg cringed when he saw the envelope from the credit card company. He knew without opening it that there was no way he could make even the minimum payment—not on what he was earning as a student worker on campus. *How did I get into this mess?* he asked himself. The answer was in the rows of charges in the statement. He had needed a couple more textbooks and new shoes; and there was that nice dinner out with Cindy. Sweat broke out on his forehead. *What do I do now? I can't work more hours and still keep my grades up. I can't ask Mom and Dad for help. And if I don't pay the minimum, they'll slap me with a late fee.* Greg wished he had never accepted the offer of a credit card! Feeling dejected, he sat down to think—and pray.

He thought of his aunt Susan. She was full of wisdom; she'd know what he should do. He decided to call her and ask.

Aunt Susan listened to Greg's dilemma. She could hear the stress in his voice. She asked him a few questions and then commented, "Greg, you're a smart young man. You have been caught in one of the devil's favorite scams—paying yourself first. A credit card isn't a bad thing unless it encourages you to spend when you don't have the money to pay the bill at the end of the month. But I think you have already experienced that.

"God wants us to put Him first, not ourselves. He says we

must 'seek first the kingdom of God and His righteousness' before we seek to fulfill our own desires. It works, Greg. I know. I've proven it."

Greg knew that his aunt spoke the truth. But how could he get out of the hole he'd dug and start over? Aunt Susan offered some suggestions. He should contact the credit card company, explain his situation, and ask them to lower the minimum payment that month. Then he should shred the credit card or put it where he couldn't get to it easily. He should commit to avoid any purchases not absolutely necessary until the card was paid off and then continue living frugally until he could build up a small bank balance. That would allow him to avoid using credit completely.

Aunt Susan paused a moment and then asked him, "Don't you have a semester break coming?" Greg said he would have a week off in two weeks. "Would you be willing to come to my house and work during spring break? I could use some help cleaning out the attic and painting the porch, and there's always plenty of yard work to do. I'll pay you if you're willing to work hard."

Greg smiled as he felt the weight lift from his shoulders. "Yes, Aunt Susan. I would love to come and help you!"

Greg said goodbye and hung up. He looked up the phone number of the credit card company and dialed the number. He was going to conquer his debt and make sure that it wouldn't haunt him again.

The Bible speaks negatively of all debt. For some people, going into debt is a vain attempt at financial success; but debt produces worry—not security. It can seem to bring temporary success, but it also results in long-term frustration and stress.

Debt tempts us to make promises we may never be able to keep, and it suggests that God can't meet all our needs. The result of debt is less money for everyday living and the emotional burden of having to pay it off in the future.

Debt is a double-edged sword. If it is not paid back, the borrower suffers financially and the unpaid loan harms the assets of the lender. Unfortunately, debt is an integral component of the world's financial system. However, we are counseled to avoid debt, and as students of the Bible we can choose not to live in debt.

Scripture clearly counsels against debt: Exodus 22:25–27; Proverbs 22:7, 26; Luke 14:28; and Romans 13:7. In order to follow this counsel and avoid debt, we must learn the habit of self-denial. Jesus said, "Whoever wants to be my disciple must deny themselves and take up their cross daily and follow me" (Luke 9:23). We think of this as a spiritual principle, and it is. But it applies to our financial life as well. "The very first lesson to be learned of Christ is the lesson of self-denial."[1] For some, this decision will have to be made daily. It is the principle of delayed gratification, and rather than spoil our fun, it will increase our happiness.

What is money?

What is money in the twenty-first century, and how does it relate to debt? We generally think that it includes coins in our pockets, paper currency in our wallets, and money in the bank. However, these are only tokens of what money really is. Money has been called a social technology that is made up of (1) "an abstract unit of value," (2) "a system of accounts" of credit or debt, and (3) value that can be transferred.

This concept has created vast fortunes and extreme poverty. It runs on greed, quick profits, usury, and deceit, and it undermines any desire for a life of self-denial. We fall in love with money. No wonder God counsels, "The love of money is a root of all kinds of evil. Some people, eager for money, have wandered from the faith and pierced themselves with many griefs" (1 Timothy 6:10, NIV).

Money, by its nature, draws a thin line between living within your income and living in debt. How we handle it is one of the most important stewardship principles we can implement on a daily basis.

Borrowing and spending

Borrowing and spending money is a vicious cycle. Unfortunately, as the foundational principle of the world's economic system, it makes materialism ubiquitous in virtually every culture on earth. However, the Bible does not support or encourage this practice as a normal way of life. You cannot stack obligation upon obligation and expect a secure outcome. Because of debt, money's own math cannot sustain itself. It's an economic system that robs the financial future as a way to promise security and stability in the present but can guarantee neither.

Going into debt affects our finances as Christian stewards more than any other action we make and has a built-in temptation to disregard disciplined financial management. "When one voluntarily becomes involved in debt, he is entangling himself in one of Satan's nets which he sets for souls."[2] While the Bible does not forbid borrowing, it strongly discourages it. If you do borrow for personal use or for advancing the cause of God, you must faithfully pay off the debt (Romans 13:7). If you are under the weight of debt, develop a plan to eliminate it as fast as possible.

Gratification

We live in a world of emotions controlled by the desire for instant gratification. This is a temptation for everyone (Psalm 73). The world offers to trade its pleasures of gratification for our birthright to heaven. Whether we go in the direction of delaying gratification or having it all now depends on our habits of self-control. The decisions we make lead us to repeated behaviors. Habits do not make us into robots, but once we make a decision, our brain has an easy path, an automatic routine that it could take again and again.

We need the fruit of the Spirit, self-control (Galatians 5:23). "Self-control is the ability to delay gratification."[3] It is well illustrated with the marshmallow experiment conducted by psychologist Walter Mischel in the 1970s. Mischel offered children a small reward immediately (one marshmallow) or a bigger reward if the child would wait fifteen minutes (two marshmallows). He and other scholars studied the lives of some of those children forty years later and found that the ones who delayed gratification had much better life outcomes, including higher grades.[4] For God's steward, delayed gratification may be a challenge, but we have help (1 Corinthians 10:13; James 1:12). Self-control is a "key factor in becoming less materialistic."[5] "The most effective way to improve your self-control is by creating an environment that sets the stage for behavioral change. Research has supported the axiom that "it is easier to avoid temptation than it is to resist it."[6]

Living within your means

Most people live from paycheck to paycheck, but those with more education tend to live within their income.[7] Do you struggle to keep your paycheck ahead of your expenses? Making the decision to live within your income is the hardest and most important money management decision you can make. This means no debt except a mortgage and possibly a vehicle that includes a payoff plan. If you never consciously decide to live debt free, you will never achieve it.

You will have a hard time living within your means if you don't use a budget. "If you are experiencing difficulty with your money management, set up a family budget. It can be as simple as totaling all your expenditures for two or three months and then averaging your monthly expenses."[8] Then compare your expenses to your income. Learn to tell your money where to go rather than asking where it went.

Saying no to debt

Solomon counsels us to never start down the road of debt (Proverbs 3:28). The Bible doesn't distinguish between good or bad debt; it simply discourages any form of it (Romans 13:8). People try to use debt as a tool to build prosperity, but more often than not, it becomes a stumbling block to spiritual growth and revival. It diverts attention from our spiritual priorities.

The best way to deal with debt is to follow this simple plan. First, "be determined never to incur another debt."[9] You must make the decision to avoid debt as if it were a contagious disease. Second, "make a solemn covenant with God."[10] Saying "no" to debt must be a spiritual decision. And third, if you already have debts, "work them off as fast as possible"[11] (Romans 13:7).

Saving and investing

If borrowing and spending is the world's philosophy, then saving and investing is the biblical perspective. Saving takes care of our needs, and investing is focused on others.

Scripture has strong words regarding the importance of providing for family and relatives (1 Timothy 5:7). Saving consistently is one way to do this. In this context, saving means taking care of all family financial responsibilities, both current and future. Consider saving for the future as a monthly expense to be paid. Put it in your budget. If the ant "stores its provisions in summer" (Proverbs 6:8), perhaps we can learn from them. "The wise store up choice food and olive oil, but fools gulp theirs down" (Proverbs 21:20).

Investing is defined in the Bible this way: "Store up for yourselves treasures in heaven" (Matthew 6:20). This will change how you look at money. "Do not work for food that spoils, but for food that endures to eternal life, which the Son of Man will give you. For on him God the Father has placed his seal of approval" (John 6:27–29). Believing in Jesus puts our possessions and our giving in the context of helping others prepare for eternity. We invest in heaven through tithe and offerings, which places our focus on helping others make a decision for eternity.

Investing is very much a part of our religious experience. It reveals to God what is in the secret chambers of our heart. "The reason that giving will always be an issue on God's agenda with us is that our generosity is one of the clearest indicators of how deeply we have drunk of the 'river of his delights' (Psalm 36:8)."[12]

If you love money, giving feels obscene. If you are in debt, giving feels impossible. But if you love God, giving is an act of grace. Nothing breaks the hold that money has over us faster than giving it away (or giving it to God's work). In the process, we can help reveal the heart of Jesus to a lost soul. Instead of feeling the burden of debt over us, we will feel the peace of heaven.

---

1. White, *Counsels on Stewardship*, 252.

2. Ibid., 254.

3. Roberts, *Shiny Objects*, 18.

4. American Psychological Association, *What You Need to Know About Willpower: The Science of Self-Control*, report, 2012, http://www.apa.org/helpcenter/willpower.aspx.

5. Roberts, *Shiny Objects*, 18.

6. Ibid.

7. Jean Chatzky, *The Difference: How Anyone Can Prosper Even in the Toughest Times* (New York: Three Rivers Press, 2009), 62, 63.

8. NAD Stewardship Department, *Faith and Finance* (Columbia, MD: North American Division, 2009), 45.

9. White, *Counsels on Stewardship*, 257.

10. Ibid.

11. Ibid.

12. Larry D. Allen, *Growing in the Grace of Giving* (Dublin, OH: Xulon Press, 2005), 21; emphasis in original.

CHAPTER 12

Habits of a Steward

Jason opened his campus mailbox and pulled out an envelope. He unfolded the note and read, "Please come to the finance office as soon as possible." It was signed by the financial officer at the university.

Jason sighed heavily. He didn't have the money to pay his school fees. He climbed the stairs to his dorm room and sank into the hard chair. The lump in his throat threatened to choke him.

Jason had grown up in a religiously divided home. His mother had become a Seventh-day Adventist when Jason was twelve, and his father was angry about it. After that, there was constant tension at home. Jason followed his mother's example and was baptized as well. His mother took a job to pay for Jason to attend the Adventist school, and when he graduated, she urged him to enroll in the Adventist university two hours away.

But then Jason's mother had become sick, and a few months later she died. Jason's father refused to pay his school fees and urged his son to transfer to the state university. Jason respectfully declined. "Then find a way to pay your school bills!" his father shouted.

Jason worked part-time off campus and was able to pay most of his expenses until the company downsized, leaving Jason without a job. While he found part-time work on campus, his school bills mounted rapidly.

Jason picked up the message from the finance office and started toward the administration building. "Lord, work a miracle for me," Jason pleaded.

"Hi, may I help you?" a pleasant student worker asked as Jason stepped up to her window.

"Yeah," Jason said without enthusiasm. "I received a note to come to the finance office. I think it's about my tuition bill." The young woman asked for his student ID number and pulled up his account on her computer. She studied the screen for a moment and then turned to a pile of receipts on her desk. "I remember this now," she said as she handed him two papers. Jason studied the first paper, a receipt, with a puzzled expression on his face. "I don't get it. This says my tuition has been paid, but I . . ."

Jason stopped speaking as the girl pointed to the second piece of paper in his hand and smiled. "It looks as if someone paid." Jason scanned the short, handwritten letter attached to the receipt. "But—but who is this person? I don't know this name."

"You *are* Jason Whitmore, aren't you?" she asked.

"Yes, but who would pay my bill when I don't even know them?" He read the letter again, more carefully this time, and found his answer. It said, "God has been speaking to me for years. Today He impressed me to send this money to be applied to Jason Whitmore's account. I'm in the habit of listening when God talks, so I know this young man needs these funds." The letter was unsigned.

Jason's heart beat fast in his chest. *Wow! God told this person exactly how much I owe on my school bill!* Then Jason read the text the unnamed donor had written at the bottom of the letter. "My God shall supply all your need according to His riches in glory by Christ Jesus" (Philippians 4:19, NKJV).

Thank You, God! he prayed. *You truly did work a miracle for me today! Thank You for Your faithfulness—and the faithfulness of this donor.*

Forming new habits

Our attitude toward God defines what kinds of decisions we will make. Right decisions are important (Proverbs 3:5, 6), and right habits are even more so (2 Corinthians 10:5; Luke 4:16). As stewards living in a chaotic world that's preoccupied with self-indulgence, where most people are pursuing their materialistic dreams, our good habits will stand out in stark contrast to those around us (John 14:23). Are we in the habit of listening to God and obeying His direction?

Charles Duhigg divides a habit into three parts: (1) the cue or trigger that puts the brain into automatic mode to let the behavior happen; (2) the routine, which is the actual behavior; and (3) the reward, a feeling the brain enjoys. This makes the "habit loop."[1] When the cue sends a signal, a decision must be made—allow the behavior to take place or stop it. The more often we make the decision that allows the behavior, the easier it is to make. With each succeeding instance, the pathway of least resistance takes over, and the behavior becomes more and more ingrained in the neuronal brain paths. The link between context and action grows stronger by repetition.

That is why old habits are so difficult to change. They are part of who you are (Psalm 119:56). New habits are hard to form but not impossible. They can form "because the brain is constantly looking for ways to save effort. Left to its own devices, the brain will try to make almost any routine into a habit, because habits allow our minds to ramp down [rest] more often,"[2] says Duhigg. Let's look at what he calls "keystone habits," because they influence the formation of other habits.

Seek God first

The first habit that stewards establish in their life is putting God first. Daniel "purposed in his heart" (Daniel 1:8, NKJV) and prayed "as was his custom" (Daniel 6:10, NKJV). He made the decision and maintained a custom. Seeking God first all the time reveals a lifestyle of one "whose delight is in the law of the LORD, and who meditates on his law day and night" (Psalm 1:2). This is not a sporadic activity but a constant one. God looks to see whether we seek Him (Psalm 53:2).

What makes us seek God first? A craving. "Cravings are what drive habits. And figuring out how to spark a craving makes creating a new habit easier."[3] On our own, well-intentioned decisions don't survive cravings. We take what the world offers, and Satan snatches our souls. We crave "heaven on earth."

Jesus sought solitude to pray early in the morning and, at other times, all night. He prayed on the cross (Luke 6:12; 23:46). The more time He spent with His Father, the more He felt that He needed it. His disciple Peter told us, "Like newborn babies, crave pure spiritual milk, so that by it you may grow up in your salvation" (1 Peter 2:2). It is what we take in and keep in the mind that makes the craving. Like the deer panting for water and the desert traveler thirsting for water (Psalm 42:1, 2; 63:1), a thirst for Him makes the craving. How badly do I want to seek God?

Look for the return of Jesus

Looking for the return of Jesus is a habit that links the context—the nearness of His coming—and the action—His glorious return. This habit protects us from being distracted by the pleasures of the world (Titus 2:12, 13). We don't know the day or hour, but we know it's soon. Each day brings us one day closer (Luke 21:28–31). Are we in the habit of looking for the second coming of Christ? (Matthew 24:42–51; Mark 13:34–37; 1 Thessalonians 5:6). If I am a steward managing God's possessions, and He is about to return, then I want to be ready and watching for that glorious event.

Make a list of the signs of Jesus' coming and fix them in your mind. Are your managerial books in order in preparation to give an account? Are you spiritually ready for that day (Matthew 25)? For this habit of mind, the cue is God's possessions, the routine is watching and managing them properly, and the reward is being with Jesus forever.

Use time wisely

God created time (Genesis 1). It is a perishable commodity that we can use any way we want, but once it is gone we can never get it back. It is one of the most important assets that stewards have to manage and is more valuable than money. Wise King David said, "Teach us to number our days, that we may gain a heart of wisdom" (Psalm 90:12). Numbering our days means being accountable for how we use our time, a God-given talent of which we have a limited supply. "Our time belongs to God. Every moment is His, and we are under the most solemn obligation to improve it to His glory. Of no talent He has given will He require a more strict account than of our time."[4]

Making a habit of managing our time has not been given the emphasis it deserves (Romans 13:11). I urge you to develop this habit by focusing on what is important in this life and the next. Habits are not engines of our minds running at idle. They are evidence of an active mind at work. "Time is one of the important talents which God has entrusted to us and for which He will call us to account. A waste of time is a waste of intellect."[5]

One of the most important habits in managing time is Sabbath observance. Sabbath is a sign of God's power. He transcends time (Joshua 10:13; Isaiah 38:8). When we keep that time holy, it shows that we acknowledge Him as the Creator and Owner of all.

How we view the Sabbath is related to our acknowledgement of who owns our possessions. "Tithing is to possessions what Sabbath is to time."[6] The Sabbath is holy, and the tithe is holy. For Sabbath to become a spiritual habit (Hebrews 10:25), we need to set the cue, which is the preparation day or sundown, and then let the spiritual routine unfold by, at least, attending Sabbath School and church. As part of our worship, we bring an offering. The reward is worshiping with believers and a day of spiritual rest that helps us look forward to heaven (Isaiah 66:23).

Living in a world where the culture pushes our emotions to govern our intellect will affect our use of time. While emotions are the energy that drives intellect, they should not govern it (1 Corinthians 2:16). Scripture teaches that intellect, rather, must govern our emotions (Jeremiah 11:20; Psalm 26:2; 1 Corinthians 9:27). To accomplish this we know that the time we have to live is short (Job 14:5) and limited (Psalm 90:10, 12), like a "mist" (James 4:14). Eternity is not easy to grasp with only our human intellect. We can't store it for the future or speed it up. But time governed by intellect means time well spent will never be lost.

Health

Health, as the saying goes, is something we don't appreciate until we don't have it. Our health habits indicate as much about our view of God as any other possession. Health comes with a particular stewardship responsibility. We are to present ourselves "as a living sacrifice, holy and pleasing to God" (Romans 12:1). "Your bodies are temples of the Holy Spirit" (1 Corinthians 6:19).

Honoring God is our motive to serve Him. "It should lead us to keep brain, bone, muscle, and nerve in the most healthful condition, that our physical strength and mental clearness may make us faithful stewards. Selfish interest, if given room to act, dwarfs the mind and hardens the heart; if allowed to control, it destroys moral power. Then disappointment comes."[7]

We must understand the relationship the mind has with the body. "Satan is the originator of disease; and the physician is warring against his work and power. Sickness of the mind prevails everywhere. Nine tenths of the diseases from which men suffer have their foundation here."[8] What our minds feed on will affect how our bodies function.

You may have heard of the five Blue Zones in the world. People in the Blue Zones live, on average, a decade longer than the rest of the population because of a healthy lifestyle for mind and body. It is not only a habit but a way of life. Loma Linda, California, is the only Blue Zone in the United States.[9] It's not a coincidence that the lifestyle of that predominantly Seventh-day Adventist city shapes its witness to the world. It is imperative that "whatever you do, do it all for the glory of God" (1 Corinthians 10:31).

Self-discipline

Someone once said that self-discipline happens when your conscience tells you to do something and you don't talk back. We are in a great struggle for self-mastery (Romans 7:15–20). Self-discipline trains the will and refines the character as we reflect Christ (2 Corinthians 7:1). Discipline is to the Christian steward what conditioning is to the runner and the boxer (1 Corinthians 9:26, 27). Business philosopher Jim Rohn said, "We must all suffer one of two things: the pain of discipline or the pain of regret or disappointment." Christ is our example in this. In Gethsemane Jesus turned the struggle of self-discipline into the greatest gift ever given (2 Peter 1:4–7). When we recognize, through Christ, a spiritual weakness, self-discipline helps us introduce a routine of doing what is right. The reward is the personal improvement of walking with God in faith.

Are we willing to make discipline a habit? "The Christian steward is no longer a servant, but a friend and a brother of his Lord. He is an ambassador of goodwill, at large, to the universe. He has told the story of redeeming love to men, he now tells it to angels."[10]

---

1. Charles Duhigg, "Habits: How They Form and How to Break Them," National Public Radio, Mar. 5, 2012, http://www.npr.org/2012/03/05/147192599 /habits-how-they-form-and-how-to-break-them.

2. Charles Duhigg, *The Power of Habit* (New York: Random House, 2012), 17, 18.

3. Ibid., 59.

4. Ellen G. White, *Christ's Object Lessons* (Washington, DC: Review and Herald®, 1941), 342.

5. White, *Testimonies for the Church*, 3:146.

6. Pete Wilson, founding and senior pastor of Cross Point Church, Nashville, TN, statement made in a presentation given at the Dave Ramsey Stewardship Conference, May 18, 2016.

7. Ellen G. White, *Messages to Young People* (Hagerstown, MD: Review and Herald®, 2002), 150.

8. White, *Testimonies for the Church,* 5:443, 444.

9. Dan Buettner, *The Blue Zones*, 2nd ed. (Washington, DC: National Geographic Society, 2012).

10. Walter M. Starks, *Principles of Christian Stewardship*, 326.

CHAPTER 13

Stewardship Outcomes

Everyone in town knew and loved Old Henry. He still lived in the house he and his wife had shared for almost fifty years, until her death. He walked more slowly these days and with a noticeable limp, but the smile on his face hadn't changed. He nursed his aging pickup into town once a week to run errands and buy groceries that almost always included a bag for someone else. After Mrs. Jacobs's husband died, she had struggled to feed and clothe her children. A couple times a month, bags of groceries appeared on her doorstep. And at Christmas the groceries accompanied a box of simple gifts for the kids. When Mr. Harold came down with pneumonia, Old Henry saw to it that the man had the medicines he needed but couldn't afford.

Children loved Old Henry, and he often stopped to talk to them or invite them to join him on his porch swing for a glass of cold water and a "grandpa" kind of chat. And if they brought him a book, he'd gladly take time to read to them.

The church received ample blessings from Old Henry too. Though he could no longer help roof the church or shovel snow, he never let an offering call pass without a generous response.

When Old Henry died, he left his home and its furnishings to his church to be used to minister in his neighborhood and beyond.

As the town's residents gathered to say goodbye to their friend, one woman mentioned that she had heard Old Henry say he had treasure hidden somewhere. When the church took possession of Henry's estate, the oversight committee obtained Old Henry's bank records. His savings account had barely a month's worth of expense money. "Perhaps he kept most of his money in his home," one member suggested. The committee agreed to keep an eye out for anything of value.

They examined each room and made notes of Old Henry's possessions. In the kitchen cupboards they found sparse supplies. They searched his bedroom and found nothing but an aging bed and a dresser with clothes. The attic held only a few boxes of photos and old clothes. After a day of careful exploring, the committee members had found nothing of monetary value. "The only thing Old Henry seemed to value was the Bible on his nightstand," the group's leader said. "By the looks of it, he must have read it for years. It is well worn and quite marked up."

Without realizing it, the committee *had* found Old Henry's secret treasure. He had given much away because he lived by the example of Christ. He was happy and content because he knew he could trust his Savior. When Old Henry had spoken of his treasure, it wasn't a box of hidden gold coins or a big bank account. It was his faith in Christ and his desire to follow Jesus in every aspect of his life.

Chaos to contentment

The world will see a successful life of stewardship in the Christian's journey of faith. Application of the principles cannot be hidden from view. The results are beneficial to us as well as to those around us.

Biblical stewardship produces a spiritual fragrance in the people who live it. Some in every generation can tell you their story of stewardship that reflects "the whole measure of the fullness of Christ" (Ephesians 4:13). There is no other way than by stewardship principles that we can move from chaos to contentment.

What are the characteristics of the successful steward?

Godliness

Before Jesus returns, some people will seem to have integrity but are really putting up a false front, "having a form of godliness but denying its power" (2 Timothy 3:5, NKJV). Godliness comes from the converted heart, an inward attitude of acceptance, a mind-set that is "on things above, not on earthly things" (Colossians 3:2). Your genuine character as a steward comes through to people as they sense the influence of your connection with Christ. God is looking for you to reveal Him in this way.

Noah, who was considered insane; Daniel, who chose the possibility of death rather than to dishonor God; and Job, who suffered intensely without knowing why—are singled out for their godly character (Ezekiel 14:14). They reflect four characteristics of a godly life. First, they were blameless (Genesis 6:9; Philippians 2:15; 1 Timothy 3:2). Second, their hearts were faithful to moral principles (Daniel 6:22). Third, they worshiped God (Job 1:20; Daniel 6:10; Genesis 8:20; Hebrews 12:28, 29). Fourth, they turned away from evil (Genesis 6:9, Job 1:1, Daniel 1:8).

These men did not have it easy, and they revealed that what you are has more influence than what you say. "The quiet, consistent, godly life is a living epistle, known and read of all men. True character is not something shaped from without, or put on: but it is something radiating from within. If true goodness, purity, meekness, lowliness, and equity are dwelling in the heart, the fact will be manifest in the character; and such a character is full of power."[1] What is truly in your heart will eventually show itself to the world.

To have someone refer to you as a godly person is the highest compliment they can give. For each of us, may it be a reflection of our true state.

The power of a godly life is a mature steward living the character of Christ, and it teaches spiritual lessons for active service (1 Timothy 4:8). Godliness is stewardship "in everyday shoe leather."[2] It is the steward's journey of faith.

Contentment

Paul describes an unsavory group of people "who think that

103

godliness is a means to financial gain" (1 Timothy 6:5). But god-liness has nothing to do with wealth. "Godliness with content-ment is great gain" (verse 6). It is the result of a relationship with Christ, in little or much, regardless of circumstances (Hebrews 13:5). Contentment in God dispels the misconception that godli-ness can be produced by materialism or its values.

Contentment is a major architectural element of stewardship that is set in place for living in a world of chaos. But contentment can be elusive. It is impossible for us to achieve on our own (John 15:5). The principle is an ongoing occupation of the Christian's heart, which has been educated for living a godly life. Our will is blended with God's will, making them one and the same.

We must understand three elements that identify true con-tentment. First, our contentment should depend on Christ in every situation. We "are led by the Spirit of God" (Romans 8:14). Second, we must understand and recognize what godly content-ment is (Psalms 16:5, 6; 23:4, 5; Acts 16:24, 25). Do not snub it or take it lightly. Third, since we were not born contented, we must learn how to be contented (Philippians 4:11, 12). Jesus said, "Take my yoke upon you and learn from me" (Matthew 11:29).

In contentment we surrender the authority over our lives to God. It's a matter of the right perspective (2 Corinthians 12:10). We may not like the learning process or the experiences that we go through, but we accept what God wants for us as He directs us.

Trust

Trust as a stewardship outcome carries a deeper meaning than just using the word interchangeably with "believe." It is a miracle. The wise Solomon instructed us, "Trust in the LORD with *all* your heart and lean not on your own understanding" (Proverbs 3:5). Trust develops over time and takes no shortcuts to God's heart. He proves Himself trustworthy as we depend on Him. Trusting in God with all our heart keeps no reserve and holds nothing back in our total commitment to Him. The only alterna-tive is to trust in finite understanding, and it is futile.

There are those who believe but do not trust. Judas believed but did not trust Christ. Abraham trusted God without reservation when he told Isaac that the Lord will provide (Genesis 22:8, 14), although on other occasions he did not do so well. Noah believed God and preached of a coming flood, and he trusted God by building and entering the ark. "Noah did everything just as God commanded him" (Genesis 6:22). The thief crucified beside Christ (Luke 23:42, 43) made a stewardship of the cross by asking for a place and trusting in Christ's response.

John Wesley's private seal contained the words *Believe-Love-Obey.* Wrap them together and you have a deeper meaning of trust. "*Love* is the heart side of *believe,* the inner side. *Obey* is the life-side of believe, the outer, the action side. . . . Obedience is the music of two wills acting together. *Believe* me, *love* me, *obey* me."[3]

The Hebrew root word for *trust* can mean "to take refuge in the Lord" (Psalm 118:8). It is not an idle mental function. Such a decision is bold but can be lost in seconds (Exodus 17:6). We must find refuge in God as we depend on the wisdom of Another. We trust by "bringing every thought into captivity to the obedience of Christ" (2 Corinthians 10:5, NKJV).

"Well done"

Stewards have not heard this commendation from Christ yet. But some day God will acknowledge before the universe the relationship His people have with Him, and their faithfulness in a world of sin, by saying, "Well done." Until then, we are strangers and pilgrims on earth, with heaven—a perfect, beautiful, and peaceful place—as our ultimate destination (Hebrews 11:13, 14).

While Jesus returns with the commendation "Well done" (Matthew 25:21) for some, others will hear a denunciation: "Depart from Me" (Matthew 7:23, NKJV). One saying brings eternal happiness, and the other utter sadness. We will not think any effort in this life was too great a sacrifice if we hear the words *well done.* But those who hear *depart from Me* will try to justify their actions (Matthew 7:22).

Christ's words *well done* are the most pleasing and satisfying words a steward will ever hear. To have unqualified divine approval expressed over our attempts to manage His possessions brings unspeakable joy, after we have done our best according to our abilities (2 Corinthians 8:12).

"When Christ's followers give back to the Lord His own, they are accumulating treasure which will be given to them when they shall hear the words, 'Well done, good and faithful servant; . . . enter thou into the joy of thy Lord.' "[4] This will be a surprise for us. We will join the singing angels as if we had known the song already. And, Jesus will "see the labor of His soul, and be satisfied" (Isaiah 53:11, NKJV).

Happiness

Happiness precedes stewardship. As a stewardship outcome it is intrinsic to everyday living. Positive psychology research describes happiness as "the experience of joy, contentment, or positive well-being, combined with a sense that one's life is good, meaningful, and worthwhile."[5] This is a quality that bridges the gap between theory and practice, based on divine principles lived out from the life of Jesus. "In order to be happy ourselves, we must live to make others happy. It is well for us to yield our possessions, our talents, and our affections in grateful devotion to Christ, and in that way find happiness here and immortal glory hereafter."[6]

Happiness follows a circular sequence. First, it appears in the steward's relationship with Christ (Proverbs 16:20). We achieve it by following a spiritual law of the mind, becoming what we most focus on (2 Corinthians 3:18). By beholding we become changed.[7] Christ rewires our brains for heaven. Second, happiness leads to success. Our happiness in Christ arises from the satisfaction of being successful at the stewardship of daily activities in work, family, health, and money. Third, success strengthens ability. Repetition of good management helps us develop further habits of stewardship. And fourth, successful stewardship increases happiness in who we are and to whom we belong. True happiness is possible only to stewards who desire nothing but Christ, seek nothing but to please Him, and exhibit it in the successful management of their actions.

These stewardship outcomes have more to do with the inner character of the person than outward emotions, although it does involve one's feelings also. Centered in Christ, each positive character trait asserts influence and complements the others, producing contentment regardless of the situation. These interrelated characteristics come from divine principles that stewards live out in a broken sinful world. This is a well-balanced life found only in Christ.

This has always been God's course of action for us. "For I know the thoughts that I think toward you, says the Lord, thoughts of peace and not of evil, to give you a future and a hope" (Jeremiah 29:11, NKJV). His plan of stewardship for us has been successful. In the last days of earth's history, can you hear God say, "Have you seen My followers, My stewards, and how they manage every aspect of life? I am their Mighty Warrior, and I take great delight in them. I rejoice at their success with singing"? (see Zephaniah 3:17). There are none like them in the universe—the people who love God and despise evil (Job 1:8). They have endured chaos and heartache, sadness and pain, but the Savior has a crown of peace waiting for them and will forever be their Friend.

---

1. Ellen G. White, *Gospel Workers* (Battle Creek, MI: Review and Herald, 1901), 243.

2. Loren Warkenton, "Godliness in Everyday Shoe Leather," Northwest Baptist Seminary, June 18, 2007, https://www.nbseminary.ca/godliness-in-everyday-shoe-leather.

3. S. D. Gordon, *Quiet Talks on John's Gospel* (New York: Fleming H Revell Company, 1915), 96.

4. White, *The Desire of Ages*, 523.

5. Sonja Lyubomirsky, *The How of Happiness: A New Approach to Getting the Life You Want* (New York: Penguin Books, 2007), Kindle edition, location 595.

6. White, *Testimonies for the Church*, 3:251.

7. White, *The Great Controversy*, 555.

Notes

Notes

Notes

Notes

Notes